NOT AN EASY TARGET

Paxton Quigley's
SELF-PROTECTION FOR WOMEN

by Paxton Quigley

Illustrated by Liz Kelsey

A FIRESIDE BOOK
Published by Simon & Schuster
New York   London   Toronto   Sydney   Tokyo   Singapore

FIRESIDE
Rockefeller Center
1230 Avenue of the Americas
New York, New York 10020

Copyright© 1995 by Paxton Quigley Enterprises, Inc.

FIRESIDE and colophon are registered trademarks
of Simon & Schuster Inc.

Designed by Irving Perkins Assoc.

Manufactured in the United States of America

1   3   5   7   9   10   8   6   4   2

Library of Congress Cataloging-in-Publication Data
Quigley, Paxton.
Not an easy target: Paxton Quigley's Self-protection for women/by Paxton
Quigley; illustrated by Liz Kelsey.
p. cm.
"A Fireside book."
Includes bibliographical references (p.   ) and index.
1. Women—United States—Crimes against—Prevention. 2.. Crime preven-
tion—United States. 3. Self-defense for women. I. Title.
HV6250.4.W65Q545 1995
362.88'082—dc20   94-39635
CIP

ISBN: 0-671-89081-6

This book contains the opinions and ideas of its author and is designed to provide useful suggestions in regard to the subject matter covered. It is sold with
the understanding that the author and publisher are not engaged in rendering
legal advice, and individuals should ascertain and abide by local, state, and federal laws regarding ownership and use of weapons and other protection devices.

The author and publisher specifically disclaim any responsibility for any liability,
loss, or risk, personal or otherwise, which is incurred as a consequence, directly
or indirectly, of the use and application of any of the contents of this book.

TO MY PARENTS,
LILLIAN RUTH AND HYMEN THEODORE MILGROM

CONTENTS

I do not wish women to have power over men; but over themselves.

——MARY WOLLSTONECRAFT,
A Vindication of the Rights of Woman, 1792

ACKNOWLEDGMENTS

NO AUTHOR WORKS completely alone. Numerous people have been helping me for years in developing my seminars as well as formulating the contents of this guide.

I especially want to thank Matthew Thomas of Model Mugging, as well as Lisa Gaeta and all of the staff at Impact Personal Safety for giving me their time and valuable insights into personal protection. Also, Julie Gottleib at *Women & Guns* magazine, who has been very helpful. Thanks also goes to Kathy Bentley, editor of *Women's Self Defense,* and Joel Poyer, editor of *Safe & Secure* magazine, who have provided me with extremely useful material. My gratitude extends to Martha Braunig at Executive Security International; Massad Ayoob at Lethal Force Institute; Don Paul, author of *Secure From Crime;* Lyn Bates and Nancy Bittle at AWARE; and Laurel Rosenberg at SAVE.

The people at Smith & Wesson have always been supportive of my work with women and I'd like to thank Ed Schultz, Bob Scott, Ken Jorgenson, and all the sales representatives. My appreciation goes to my business colleagues and friends, Barrie Lynn, Nancy Moran Sanchez, and Nancy Sarnoff. I am grateful to Tom Fredericks at Bianchi, Mike Dillon at Dillon Precision, Bob Coyle at Lew Horton, and Les Whitney and Bill Baker at

Pachmayr. Special thanks go to John Fulton, Ben Hambleton, and Jodi Root at Intertrade Marketing.

Particular thanks to Joe Bowland, Barbara Brandt, Pam and Tom Ehret, Christine O'Mara, Mary Rybka, Michele Sullivan, and Kathryn Williams, as well as the good people at Orange County Shooting & Training Center, Long Beach Pistol Range, Angeles Shooting Ranges, and Huntington Beach Police Range for helping me with my seminars in Southern California.

Also, my appreciation to Dan Schrier and Susan Winston for their media expertise as well as Dale Lang, publisher of *Working Woman,* and Ted Charron and Norm Schwartz of Charron, Schwartz & Partners for their advertising savvy. My gratitude extends to members of the media, who have been most kind to me.

To my parents and to my sons, a special thanks for their love and encouragement. And to friends Allen Baron, Barbara Cohn, David Columbia, Marshall Grode, Jeffrey Mannix, John Sack, Phil Sims, and Marie Yates for their long-time support and friendship.

I would like to thank my editor, Kara Leverte, for her dedication to helping women protect themselves. Also, my appreciation goes to my agent, Stan Corwin, who is also a good friend.

Most of all I want to thank David Carnoy. Without him, this book would never have been written. His ideas and editing talent helped shape the tone and contents of the book.

Finally, I want to thank all of my students who have helped me learn so much about personal protection and, particularly, the meaning of women's empowerment.

INTRODUCTION

FOR MUCH OF my adult life, I made little effort to learn how to protect myself against a possible criminal attack. I took Kenpo Karate classes, but mainly for sport, listened to a couple of lectures on self defense, and heeded the advice my parents had given me as a child: Be careful who you talk to and don't visit certain places alone, especially after dark. It was a simple philosophy and seemingly an effective one, because I'd never been the victim of a serious crime.

But then, eight years ago, something happened that made me reevaluate my outlook. Early one morning—it was about two A.M.—I was woken up by a call from a friend who lived nearby. "Pax," she said in a strained voice I'll never forget, "someone broke into my home. The police are here. I need to talk to you. Would you mind coming over?"

When I got there, it was clear that more than a break-in had taken place. My friend's cheek was cut and badly bruised, and one eye was practically swollen shut. Her clothes were also torn.

"Did he rape her?" I quietly asked one of the police officers.

"Yes," the officer said.

Only later, when we were in the hospital, waiting for a doctor to examine my friend, did she tell me the full story. The attacker, she said, had broken in through the bathroom window on the second floor. She awoke to that sound—the glass shattering—and, after a moment's hesitation, decided to run downstairs, where she could escape through the front door. But the man was fast. He grabbed her at the top of the stairs and hit her in the face, knocking her to the ground. He kept hitting her and then forced himself on top of her.

"It didn't take long," she said. "It didn't take long at all."

Like me, her self-protection strategy had always been to avoid trouble by being prudent. Though she'd had fears of being raped—she'd had nightmares about it—she never believed she could become a victim.

"Part of me always thought that if I didn't have violent thoughts or hurt anybody physically or emotionally, no one would hurt me," she explained to me a few days after the attack. "I just thought, you know, that my good karma would protect me."

Until that day, I, too, often rationalized that my "good karma" would keep me from becoming a victim. But after my friend was raped, I realized that was ridiculous and vowed to take action. Over the next couple of weeks, I installed better door locks in my home, a house alarm system, and an exterior motion detector lighting system. I also worked up my courage to take a private handgun lesson at the Beverly Hills Gun Club. It was a difficult, soul-searching decision, because I had long been an advocate for strong gun control legislation, but I felt I had to examine all the options.

None of my friends owned a gun, and when I told them I was thinking of buying one, they were shocked. "Don't you think you're going a little overboard?" one friend asked.

No, I didn't. "Today's criminal," I said, "has no respect for human life. It used to be that criminals just took your money, then left. But now they'll shoot or stab you for no reason at all. They're cowards."

Intrigued by my change of heart, I began to research the subject of women and guns and found that there were more than 12 million American women who owned guns, but virtually nothing had been written on the topic. So I decided to do the writing myself. I sent publishers a book proposal, and after a number of rejections, E.P. Dutton offered me a contract. Eighteen months later, *Armed & Female* was published.

For the book, I interviewed over 100 rape victims as well as convicted rapists at San Quentin Penitentiary. I also attended the best gun courses and self-defense schools, including two bodyguard schools.

Armed & Female was and still is a controversial book. As a result, the media has taken an interest in me, and I have appeared on numerous radio and television shows, including "60 Minutes," "The Today Show," "Good Morning America," and the "NBC Nightly News." The media as well as the public are responding to the overwhelming presence of violence toward women. People are afraid of becoming victims and angry that nothing is being done to make their streets safe.

Not long after *Armed & Female* was published, I was approached by Ted Stermer, the president of the Orange County Shooting and Training Center, an outdoor range in Santa Ana, California. He asked me if I would instruct an all-day seminar for women on personal protection and the use of handguns. I accepted his offer, seeing it as a natural extension of my book, and began to plan a curriculum.

Initially, I designed the course to teach women how to fire and feel comfortable using handguns. But then, as I began to realize that even a gun had its limitations—in certain situations, for example, you wouldn't be able to get to your gun—I started to incorporate other self-defense strategies in my seminar, including nonlethal weapons, and awareness techniques that helped my students learn how not to become targets. I also taught them verbal and physical self-defense exercises.

I called the seminar Women's Empowerment in the '90s. The name comes from a word that I kept hearing my students use after they took the course. I would receive phone calls and letters from graduates who said they felt "empowered" in their daily lives. My students' husbands even called to tell me that their wives had changed, and they, too, used the word *empowered*.

One of my students, a young mother of two children, explained to me, "Before I took the seminar, I used to be afraid when I was out with my kids. I felt that if something happened, I wouldn't know how to handle the situation. Since taking the seminar, I now know what I would do, especially with my kids. After the course, I felt a slow change come over me. I started feeling more self-assured. I carried myself differently, even the way I walked changed."

A student from southern California, who is in her fifties, wrote me that "learning how to protect myself changed me in the sense that I have a quiet powerful feeling that I can take care of myself, especially in my home. That's a feeling of empowerment. My husband is especially happy that he doesn't have to worry about me if he isn't home. He even tells his friends that I'm empowered."

Another student, a marketing specialist, explained that she now has a set of guidelines and rules to govern herself. "Before the class, my life wasn't my own. People were always telling me what to do and what not to do. Now, I know what I want and what's right for me, and I don't necessarily take their advice. For me, that's been a great step in my life. I feel in control and that means empowerment to me."

Most of the graduates who described their emerging empowerment were successful in their work and in their family relationships, but they said that prior to the seminar, they all endured a quiet terror that bordered on phobia, especially when they were out alone at night. Once they talked about it, they understood that much of their fear emanated from not knowing what to do if they were in imminent danger. After discussing this fear with my students as well as other women, I realized that even though a woman might have had a well-paying job, owned a home or condominium, and had a satisfying relationship with a husband or a significant other, she was not really empowered if she was *scared* when she walked on the street, drove her car, or slept in her home. Fear, and particularly fear for her own safety, stopped her from realizing a full life.

Certainly, the New Age philosophers and the women's movement leaders have helped to enhance the consciousness and confidence of women, both on an economic and a social level, but these well-intentioned spokespeople have not addressed women's real fears and given them a set of personal protection strategies to follow in an unsafe world.

Clarissa Pinkola Estés in her best-selling book, *Women Who Run with the Wolves,* invites women to recognize that the "most vital and interesting part of themselves—the part that is earthy and instinctual—has been all but snuffed out by nonstop demands from the family, the workplace, and themselves."

Marianne Williams in *A Woman's Worth* tells women to treat themselves like queens instead of second-class citizens or slave girls.

Camille Paglia in *Sex, Art and American Culture* writes that "it is a woman's personal responsibility to be aware of the dangers of the world."

All of these feminists encourage women to discover their own paths to becoming whole people, but they have left out one crucial element: A woman cannot become completely self-reliant if she doesn't learn how to protect herself.

Studies have shown that women who escape assault exhibit two traits: (1) They are cautious and aware of their environment and (2) they are mentally and physically prepared to put up resistance. In my class, I tell my students that some of these traits are instinctual but that others have to be learned. The key to becoming empowered is developing your own personal survival strategy. Each of you must find your strategy, define it, and always carry it with you.

It is my hope that the information and advice I offer in this book will enable you, the reader, to develop a personal survival strategy that will allow you to discover freedom and empowerment. Not all of this advice will apply to you, and some of it may sound extreme, but what's important is that you come out feeling more aware of the world you live in and more confident in your ability to defend yourself against the dangers that world possesses. Only then can you become responsible for your own safety.

CHAPTER ONE

Who Is the Enemy?

A MINORITY OF MEN perpetrate violence against women. It's not a new phenomenon. It's been going on for decades, centuries, and perhaps since the beginning of humankind.

What is surprising is that these men make up a smaller segment of the male population than you might think. The problem is a relatively small number of men are committing a lot of crimes. A Bureau of Justice study estimated that only 6 percent of the criminals who are considered violent offenders committed 70 percent of all the violent crimes in the United States in 1992. According to a study done by the National Victim Center in 1992, a rapist attacks an average of seven different victims before being captured.

Only in the last twenty years has the subject of violence against women been seriously reported, addressed, and debated in America. There is no consensus as to why this violence is occurring. Some authorities blame the increase on TV, movie, and video game violence. Others attribute it to the loss of family values and increased parental neglect and abuse brought on by drug and alcohol abuse. But if all of these factors were valid, we would see substantial increases in female violence, but that isn't happening. According to the FBI's Uniform Crime Reports, from 1966 to 1987, the percentage of women committing

violent crimes increased only 2.1 percent (9 to 11.1 percent).
Another explanation, which is highly controversial but gaining credence among some members of the medical and scientific community, is that men who are habitual offenders—serial rapists, serial child molesters, and murderers—may have violence ingrained in their genes.

In a 1993 *Time* magazine article, Gregory Carey, an assistant professor at the University of Colorado's Institute for Behavioral Genetics, said, "In virtually every behavior we look at, genes have an influence—one person will behave one way, another person will behave another way. It stands to reason that genes might contribute to violent activity as well."

Dutch and American researchers created quite a stir in 1993 when they reported in the journal *Science* that they had linked violent behavior in men to a tiny defect in the gene that enables the body to produce an enzyme called MAOA (monoamine oxidase a). MAOA "breaks down the molecules that transmit signals inside the brain." Men with this gene mutation don't produce MAOA, so their brains have a high percentage of the chemical molecules serotonin, dopamine, and noradrenaline, which stimulate erratic, aggressive behavior. The gene is located on the X chromosome, which explains why only males, with their single copy of the X chromosome, can suffer from the enzyme deficiency. Interestingly, women can be carriers of the genetic defect, but they are protected from its symptoms because they possess a second, good copy of the gene, which sits on their second X chromosome.

The *Houston Chronicle* reported that "the [Dutch and American] researchers do not yet know how many people worldwide may suffer from the enzyme deficiency, but based on other types of hereditary disorders, they estimate that defects in monoamine oxidase-a are likely to afflict no more than one in 100,000 people."

Twenty years ago, there wasn't as great a need to learn self-protection. Not only was crime comparatively low, but there weren't as many women in the workforce as there are today. Nor did they travel as much. These changes have forced women to face a whole new set of problems, many of which have left them feeling insecure and vulnerable.

You may find it easier to live with your fear or simply bury it. I used to hide it from myself. So did many of my students. But only when you confront it and realize who and what your real enemies are, will it begin to disappear.

Who Are the Muggers, Burglars, and Carjackers?

If you are targeted by a criminal, he will probably be between the ages of eighteen and twenty-four, unemployed, and most likely on drugs. The U.S. Department of Justice reports that, for example, 40 percent of burglars are under the influence of crack cocaine while committing a crime. In regards to race, specifically in the category of homicide, FBI statistics show that if you are Afro-American, you are more apt to be murdered by an Afro-American than by anyone else. And if you are white, you are more likely to be murdered by a white person than by anyone else.

A criminal may work alone, with a partner (who may be a female), or with multiple partners. He may be well dressed, appear nonthreatening, and not look like the stereotypical criminal that is so often portrayed on television. According to Louis R. Mizell, Jr., in his book, *Street Sense for Women,* "criminals use some form of deception, somewhere along the line, in 90 percent of their operations; a trick, ruse, disguise, ploy, prop, or false story. . . . And it is important to know that in literally thousands of cases, a collection of con artists, kidnappers, rapists, and robbers have preceded their crime with one of three questions: 'May I use your telephone?', 'Do you have the time?', and (asking directions) 'Can you tell me how I get to . . .?' "

The criminal working the streets is more violent than ever before and is not troubled by the consequences of his actions. Many of today's criminals have no feeling or remorse for other people's suffering. After holding up a person, he thinks nothing of killing his victim.

When crack cocaine became popular in the late 1970s, police began seeing a greater percentage of women and men being murdered during street and home robberies, carjackings, and other confrontations. Sergio Robleto, who heads the Los Angeles Police Department's South Bureau homicide division, explains that "in previous decades, many of the property crimes were committed by heroin addicts who were low-key and docile and favored burglaries. But crack addicts are more edgy and paranoid . . . people who will pull holdups and carjackings and can kill very quickly."

Two things have happened to make people more fearful. First, there is no longer the widespread belief that police and courts can protect you. This makes people more frightened and gives crime sort of the character of cancer. It can happen any time and no one can protect you. The second thing is that the character of crime has changed. Crime is teen-age, it's impulsive, it's irrational. Doing injury is the purpose. . . . It's like getting hit by lightning.

—Gerald M. Caplan, dean, McGeorge Law School, Sacramento, California, *Los Angeles Times,* December 6, 1993, p. A12

Who Are the Rapists?

The following article was printed in the *Los Angeles Times* on December 6, 1993:

> The trial of a Westlake man who authorities say was among the most active rapists in Los Angeles history began Monday with the prosecution and defense attorney arguing whether a single suspect was responsible for the 17 sexual assaults in question. . . . Fuentes, 33, described as a religious, family-loving man by police, has pleaded not guilty to all 56 felony counts on which he is being tried, including the multiple charge of rape, attempted rape, forcible oral copulation and sodomy. . . . Police say the Salvadoran native was a leading suspect in 27 other rapes for which charges were never filed because the victims—mainly poor Latinas—were unwilling to testify, fearing that their families would disown them. Detectives said there may have been dozens of other victims who never reported their rapes during a series of sexual assaults from 1989 to 1992.

When you picture a rapist, you probably don't think of a man like Mr. Fuentes. Several of my students have told me they have had nightmares about a "scummy" man who rapes or tries to rape them. He is a loner—unemployed, uneducated, and possibly homeless. But in reality, a rapist has no defined look or socioeconomic background. Often, he has a wife or girlfriend and maybe children. He may work and socialize easily and have above-average intelligence. He may be black; he may be white. He may be a doctor, lawyer, clergyman, businessman, or even the man who lives next door to you.

Authorities don't know what causes a man to become a rapist, although studies show that a high percentage of rapists were sexually abused as children. However, Dr. Park E. Dietz, one of the country's leading experts on rapists, says that it's too simplistic to blame childhood abuse. In a *Washington Post* interview, Dietz explains that "[rapists'] sexual desires are learned through personal experience and media exposure. Their willingness to act criminally for the sake of an orgasm comes from bad genes and bad parenting."

High Recidivism Among Rapists

Whatever the reasons are, law enforcement officials and psychiatrists admit that the recidivism rate among rapists is high. Statistics show that an incarcerated rapist will spend less than three years in prison and 52 percent of convicted rapists will be rearrested within three years of probation.

Fred Berlin, director of the National Institute for the Study, Prevention and Treatment of Sexual Trauma in Baltimore, Maryland, says that repeat rapists are similar to alcoholics in that "they can be *treated* but not often cured." He claims to have had success in treating rapists with a combination of medication and behavioral therapy. After he finishes administering his treatment at his private clinic, Berlin continues to monitor his patients, and he says that after five years only 5 of his patients out of 100 have gone on to commit another rape. Yet he cautioned that the patients who had remained trouble-free were not cured but had only learned to *control* their impulses.

The recidivism rate of the sex offender is almost 80%. But when the parole boards meet, the sex offender is the most likely to be paroled because they are often considered non-violent. Thus we, as police officers, are forced to see the results of this insane practice of treating some of the most violent, dangerous men as if they were Vienna choirboys.

—Lieutenant Brenda Maples, Tennessee Police Department, Memphis president, the Law Enforcement Alliance of America

---

Rapists who have undergone therapy report that they enjoy the power they wield over their victims and often get more aroused planning and revising their crime than from the actual rape. One rapist in an FBI study conducted by Roy Hazelwood, an expert in the behavioral patterns of serial rapists at the FBI's Behavioral Science Services Unit in Quantico, Virginia, explained that after he broke into a woman's home, he would quietly stand at her bed and silently count to ten before raping her. He said he was "putting off the rape" because it was the "least enjoyable part of the whole thing." Asked why he didn't stop and leave, he responded, "Pardon the pun, but after all I had gone through to get there, it would have been a crime not to rape her."

A groundbreaking study done by Groth and Birnbaum in the 1970s has led Hazelwood as well many experts in the field to break sexual assault down into three distinct categories: *power* rape, *anger* rape, and *sadistic* rape.

Power rape is the most common rape. The rapist seeks power and control over the woman. He intimidates her with a weapon and threatens to harm her but rarely uses excessive force to accomplish his goal of rape. This type of rapist usually feels inadequate in life, and the rape gives him a temporary feeling of power.

The assault is premeditated, and according to Gary Lowe, a specialist with the California State Department of Corrections' Sex Offender Program, these men usually attack someone their own age but have trouble maintaining an erection.

In contrast to the power rapist, the anger rapist expresses his anger, rage, and hatred by raping. His sexual assaults are brutal and usually involve beatings or making the victim perform degrading acts. Often, the victim will be sodomized or penetrated with foreign objects. These men, according to Groth and Birnbaum, use "far more force . . . than would be necessary if the intent were simply to overpower the victim."

Anger assaults are usually episodic and are often triggered by an emotional problem the man has with a woman whom he considers significant. He'll think she has rejected him or put him down in some way and go out and rape a stranger in "revenge." Lowe says that this type of rapist gets very little sexual satisfaction during a rape and often rapes elderly women.

An anger rapist can become a sadistic rapist, who is by far the most dangerous rapist. For the sadistic rapist, the act of aggression becomes eroticized, and the rape usually ends in homicide.

In a speech given at a conference on serial killers and mass murderers at the University of Windsor in Canada, Hazelwood said that serial rapists who go on to commit murder usually display four behavioral patterns in their early attacks:

1. They abduct their victims and drive them to another location before assaulting them and letting them go.
2. The attacks usually involve bondage, such as tying the victim's hands.
3. They perform anal sex on the victims.
4. They keep the women in captivity for at least twenty-four hours before releasing them.

"Whenever I find all four of these behaviors in a rape case, the hairs on the back of my neck go straight up," Hazelwood said in the speech. He contended that the majority of men who rape will continue to rape until they are captured. "I'm not certain there's any such thing as a nonserial rapist," Hazelwood said. "I think what happens is that some of these individuals get caught before they become serial rapists."

He also pointed out that there is no national system for tracking repeat sexual offenders. In his research for the FBI study, he found forty-one men who were responsible for more than 1,200 rapes and attempted rapes. This made him question whether there were more rapists on the loose or just more "stranger rapes" being done by a small number of men. Although the number of reported rapes grew by 35 percent from 1982 to 1991, Hazelwood said that law enforcement doesn't know whether it was a rise in the number of serial rapists or increased reporting that was responsible for the rise in rape.

The Three Approaches to Sexual Assault

According to Hazelwood, there are three general approaches to the rape attack. The one most often used is the *con approach,* where a rapist passes himself off as a policeman, security guard, repairman, or delivery man. He'll talk to a woman for a while, gaining her confidence and access to her home or business before he attacks her.

With the *blitz approach,* the rapist targets a woman, then physically assaults her when he finds her alone in a public facility or walking or jogging outside.

The *surprise approach* usually refers to an attack that takes place in a woman's home at night. The rapist quietly enters the home and sneaks up on the woman, who is asleep. She may wake up to the feeling of a hand over her mouth or a knife or gun pressed to her skin. The man tells her to be quiet, threatens to kill her, then rapes her. He then leaves without doing any further damage.

The Five T's:
The Modus Operandi of Criminals

As you can see, a criminal attack is rarely a random attack. Law enforcement officials and various researchers have studied the behavioral patterns of assailants and have identified five different stages in an assault.

The following are the Five T's, which I have adapted from materials written by the Women's Institute for Self Empowerment:

1. *Target.* This is when the attacker, whether a burglar, rapist, mugger, or child molester, selects his victim. It can take minutes; hours; or, in the case of a stalker, days, weeks, or months. He is looking for a person who he considers vulnerable. That person may appear physically or psychologically weak, lost, or nervous or may be predictable in her habits. He will often eliminate some women he finds unsuitable.

2. *Test.* This is the time the assailant assesses whether the potential victim is an easy target. To see how she reacts, he will usually interact in a seemingly innocent way with her, maybe asking for directions or the time of the day. Sometimes he'll follow or stare at her or even bump into her. His main goal is to enter the woman's physical and psychological space to determine how she will respond. This interval can take seconds, minutes, or even an hour.

3. *Threaten.* At this point, he has chosen his victim and he wants to overpower her. The violence escalates by intimidation and humiliation. He may verbally abuse her or threaten her with bodily harm; he may say he has a weapon or brandish one. (Weapons are used in only 25 percent of rapes and attempted rapes. Knives are used in

about 12 percent of the rapes and guns in 10 percent of the rapes.)

4. *Touch.* This is when the assault takes place, whether it's a carjacking, mugging, kidnapping, or rape. Usually, other forms of aggression may occur such as being choked, punched, or dragged.

5. *Takeoff.* After the assault, the assailant may become nervous or even feel guilty and turn his feelings into further violence. At this stage, there is a high probability—up to 80 percent—that the woman may be beaten, mutilated, or murdered.

As you can see, each stage becomes more violent, which means trying to prevent the attacker from moving on to the next stage is vital. Hopefully, by following the suggestions in the following chapters, you can avoid becoming a target and prevent an attack before it ever happens.

Crime Statistics

According to the FBI, Americans—for the first time—are more likely to be killed by a stranger than by a family member or friend. "Every American now has a realistic chance of being murdered because of the random nature the crime has assumed," says the FBI's Uniform Crime Report for 1993. In a study of homicide patterns, strangers and unknown killers made up 53 percent of the cases. FBI Director, Louis Freeh, called the nation's crime rate "unacceptably high."

Source: *USA Today*, December 5, 1994, Page 1.

CHAPTER TWO

Your Personal Survival Strategy

YOUR PERSONAL SURVIVAL strategy is not something you turn on or off or pull out of your purse when you need to. Unfortunately, it's not that simple. Your personal survival strategy has to be on all the time. It has to be a way of life.

Your personal survival strategy, or PSS, is composed of three dynamics: awareness, boundary setting, and resistance. Some people liken these dynamics to street smarts or a don't-mess-with-me attitude, but they are much more than that. Your PSS not only incorporates measures that will keep you from becoming a target but actual fighting techniques that can help you escape a violent situation. It is present when you deal with people in a business or social setting, when you walk on the street, drive your car, or use public transportation. It will also help you create a safer home and workplace.

If particular care and attention is not paid to the ladies, we are determined to foment a rebellion and will not hold ourselves bound by any laws in which we have no voice or representation.

—Abigail Adams, 1776

Awareness

Becoming more aware can be difficult at first, because it usually means confronting fears, in particular, fears of becoming a victim and not knowing how to protect yourself. Many women avoid their fears by saying, "Well, nothing bad will happen to me. I'm careful." That's true—you may be careful—but it's a big mistake to think that being careful instantly makes you safe. These days, careful isn't good enough, and that's a hard thing for many women to accept.

So, it's important to admit to yourself that you're scared. One of the best ways to do that is to simply write your safety anxieties down on a piece of paper or talk to a friend. I'll never forget the time years ago when I confessed to a male friend that I actually dreaded coming home alone at night because I had to park my car in my garage and walk approximately 100 feet to the front door of my house. I hated those 100 feet, I told him, even though telling him made me feel exposed and vulnerable. I expected him to sympathize with me, but he just said, "Well, then, do something about it. There's no reason you should have to feel that way."

Your awareness is directly tied to your ability to be a good observer. Some people are better at this than others. They are often described as "perceptive" or "more attuned to detail." But most of the time, there is a reason for this. They are good observers or they have a trained eye. So there's no reason you can't become more aware. You just have to become a better observer and learn how to watch people and take stock of your surroundings.

However, you shouldn't think that becoming an observer makes you paranoid or robotic. On the contrary, being an observer can actually be a pleasurable experience. For instance, many people like to sit at outdoor cafés and other places and "people-watch." It is quite relaxing and actually a good way to develop your awareness.

The Objective Observer

By becoming a good observer, you can learn to quickly assess a situation and a person's behavior. If it seems threatening, you can then choose a strategy that will allow you to escape that situation unharmed.

I'll give you an example. Before taking my seminar, Lois Silverstein, a student of mine, was robbed in front of her house by a man who followed her home from the supermarket. She actually saw him loitering in front of the supermarket but thought nothing of it. She walked to her car, loaded her groceries in the trunk, and then drove to her home, which was two miles from the store. She parked her car in the driveway as she normally did but when she got out of the car, she looked up and saw a man coming toward her with a knife. She froze.

"Gimme your money and shut up," he said, pressing the blade to her throat.

Fortunately, he only wanted to rob her and ended up taking the $100 or so she had in her purse and driving off in his own car without harming her.

"I was glad something worse didn't happen," she said. "But I felt humiliated because I'd seen him earlier. I should have known."

She should have and probably would have had she been a better observer. Instead of walking directly to her car, she should have stopped for a moment outside the entrance to the supermarket and assessed the situation. She should have given the parking lot and the sidewalk in front of the market a quick scan and checked to see who was around. When she saw the man who appeared to be loitering, she should have looked him directly in the eye and made him aware that she had seen and registered him.

She could have done two things next. She could have gotten in her car and made sure he didn't follow her, or if she felt uncomfortable even walking to her car, she could have gone back inside the supermarket and told the manager about the man out front. The manager could walk her out to her car and after she left, he could keep an eye on the man out front or even speak to him.

On her way home, she should have looked in her rearview mirror and made sure she wasn't being followed. Also, after she arrived at her house and parked her car, she should have scanned the immediate area and made sure it was clear.

Had she taken these steps and employed these observational skills, she might have been safe and $100 richer.

Assessing the Situation

As a trained observer, you're constantly assessing your surroundings. If you do find yourself in a dangerous situation, your observational skills will help you analyze the force you're being threatened with and the risks you'll take resisting that force. Immediately, you'll ask yourself a series of questions: Does your attacker have a gun, knife, or other makeshift weapon, such as a screwdriver or other blunt instrument? How close is he to you? Is he blocking you in such as way that you can't escape? Is he under the influence of alcohol or drugs? (Often, you can tell by his speech or the way his eyes look.) What is his emotional state? Is he angry, irrational, paranoid, nervous, or confused? What are his physical characteristics? Is he jittery or is he steady and cautious? What is he saying? Is he threatening to harm you? Is he loud and angry? Is he soft-spoken but determined?

After you answer these questions, you'll turn your attention to other details. Are there people around so that you can yell? Can you flee? If you're indoors, are there windows or doors that are accessible for escape? Are there makeshift weapons around, like loose dirt, rocks, or bottles that you can use?

Assessment Drill

The assessment I described above can be done in seconds, especially if you've practiced evaluating situations in a safe and comfortable setting. Next time you're at a shopping mall, airport, subway station, or sporting event, sit down on a bench and watch people for a while. When you can, discreetly target someone and watch their actions and identify their emotions and physical characteristics. Then, when you're satisfied you've made a thorough assessment, go on to another target. After a while, you'll begin to pick up various visual and verbal cues and be more adept at assessing people. Just for the fun of it, guess their emotions, imagine who they are, what they do, and where they're going.

In addition, imagine what you would do if a gunman entered your office (or another building you are in) and started firing. Where would you go? What exit would you use? Is there anything on your desk you could use as a weapon or a shield?

This may sound extreme, but I've had students tell me they've asked themselves similar questions, especially after they read about a gunman's rampage in the newspaper. "I sometimes wonder what I would have done if I had been in the victims' shoes and I look around my office and my imagination gets going," said one student.

After you do this drill, you may also want to take a moment to assess yourself and the clothes you are wearing. Certain clothes, especially tight skirts, long dresses, and high-heeled shoes can restrict your movements and make it difficult for you to flee quickly. Practice running in your work shoes, especially if you wear high heels. Can you run? If you find that you're having trouble, and most women do, then change into a pair of sneakers or other low-heeled shoes just before you leave the office.

Personal Boundaries

Boundaries exist on many different levels. In a larger context, countries have their own boundaries, which we call *borders*. Other countries don't violate these borders unless they're going to war. Animals, too, have their own territorial boundaries and will fight to retain them.

Every human being has boundaries. First, there are cultural boundaries, which differ from country to country or religion to religion. For example, in France, most people won't ask you what you do when you first meet them. It's just not done. It's not considered proper. But in the United States, one of the first questions people ask each other is, What do you do? It's culturally acceptable to ask.

Your personal boundaries are typically set by family upbringing. Unfortunately, some parents, grandparents, or other caregivers have had their boundaries damaged by their forefathers and have no sense of a child's personal space. Their behavior can range from small indiscretions, like reading a child's mail without her permission or listening in on her phone conversations, to larger ones, like entering a bedroom or bathroom without knocking or, in extreme instances, physically abusing or sexually molesting a child.

If you're brought up with an ill-defined sense of your personal boundaries, as an adult, you may unknowingly permit other people—both friends and strangers—to violate your inherent human boundaries. You may become sexually promiscuous or have a hard time having close relationships. Other reactions may include being a people pleasurer and not being able to say no when you mean no. Similarly, you may also allow people to verbally abuse you.

Most women aren't exactly sure of their boundaries. They don't know when to say yes or no or to assert themselves.

Boundary Setting

Watch two people when they're talking to each other. If you're in the United States, you'll notice that they're probably standing about an arm's length apart. In Europe, it's a little closer, but in the United States, an arm's length 360 degrees around your body is considered your physical boundary. There is no law that says you have to stay out of a person's physical space, but most people do stay out unless they're invited in.

I like to tell my students to think of this boundary as an invisible shield that's an extension of their mental and physical strength. Unless someone has a gun, it's very difficult for them to harm you if you keep them outside your boundary. That's why it's extremely important to maintain your boundary.

For example, a man stops a woman in a shopping mall and politely asks her for the time. He may even stick his hand out and stop her. What should she do? If she looks down at her watch and takes her eyes off him, there is a chance he will use this distraction to take advantage of her in some way.

Well, depending on your assessment of the situation, you can do one of three things.

1. If you feel safe and there are a number of other people around, you can back away from him a little, look down at your watch, and tell him the time.

2. You can keep walking and not say anything—ignore him.
3. Keep walking but say you don't know what time it is or give him an approximate time.

The important thing is that all three responses allow you to maintain your physical space, diminishing the possibility that something bad will happen to you. It is never too late to begin to set your own boundaries in a way that feels comfortable and doesn't alienate family members, friends, or business associates. You don't have to do it instantly. The first step is to start watching your own behavior with strangers.

Boundary Setting Drills

To build up your confidence in boundary setting, practice the following exercises:

1. Stand in front of a full-length mirror, raise your strong hand, and yell "Stand back" or "Stay away." Make sure that you're giving a strong command. Do this three times for the next four days.
2. Then ask a male friend to come to your home and have him stand five feet away from you and walk into your physical space. While he is coming toward you, attempt to stop him. Tell him to stand back or stay away. At first, he should back off, but as you continue to do the exercise, he should resist your commands and only heed them when he feels that you really mean it. Do these exercises at least ten times.
3. Next, do exercise 2 again but this time outside, where you probably feel less comfortable. Do this exercise at least ten times.

4. Finally, ask your male friend to have one of his friends you don't know take his place. That way, you can practice doing the drills with a stranger.

BODY LANGUAGE

Consciously or unconsciously, we form immediate impressions about people based on their physical presence. *The first aspect of assertive behavior is body language.*

1. Does someone appear comfortable—or uneasy, purposeful—or confused, confident—or intimidated?
2. Does she expand into the space around her or shrink into as little space as possible?
3. How does she hold her head . . . erect or cast downward?
4. Does she avert her eyes or maintain eye contact?
5. How is her posture? Straight or with hunched shoulders?
6. Where are her hands? Behind her back, swinging at her sides, in her pockets, on her hips?
7. If she is standing still, what is her stance? Legs apart, legs crossed, in balanced position?
8. If she is walking, how is her stride? Firm, hesitant, brisk, slow?
9. If she is sitting, does she fill the chair or draw her limbs in around her?
10. It has been estimated that up to 90 percent of our communication with other people is *non*verbal! No matter what your mouth may be saying, if it is not backed up with congruent body language, your verbal message will be discounted.

Permission to print granted by BAMM Impact, San Carlos, California.

"Back off!" yells a woman who is doing a boundary setting exercise with her friend to help build her assertiveness.

Resistance

If you can retreat from a potentially dangerous situation, retreat. That means running away and yelling to draw attention to the attacker.

However, if you're trapped by an attacker and don't feel you can get away, you need to resist. There are various forms of resistance. If you sense that you have time on your side, you should attempt to verbally deescalate the situation. Deescalating is a soft form of resistance. Yelling commands or obscenities or fighting are hard forms of resistance.

I'm sure that you've been in a nonviolent argumentative situation and found that if you can communicate your feelings to someone or calm a person down—whether he or she is a business associate or friend—you can deescalate the situation so it isn't as volatile. You can employ the same strategy in a dangerous confrontation.

However, it's very difficult to talk to a highly agitated or angry man in a calm and commanding manner, especially if he has a gun or knife. It's not impossible, though. I have heard numerous stories of women who have convinced their would-be attackers to leave and not rape them. Many of the women lied. Some said they were having their periods or had cancer or AIDS. Others said their boyfriend was coming home at any moment. One woman offered her attacker a cup of coffee and said if he left after he finished it, she wouldn't report him. Another asked her attacker how he would feel if this were happening to his sister or mother.

Other women have used other tactics. They've feigned epileptic seizures. They've fainted. They've vomited or urinated. Their attackers actually became frightened or disgusted and left before harming them.

These soft resistance responses are more effective if you know the attacker. If you're attacked by a stranger, in most instances, you won't have the time to try these tactics. In the end, though, even if you know the attacker, be prepared to physically resist. Study after study indicates that a woman is less likely to be raped if she puts up some form of resistance.

Later, I will go into more detail, describing how you can resist using various forms of verbal and physical self-defense, but for now I think it's important for you to keep in mind what will make up the main elements in your Personal Survival Strategy: awareness, boundary setting, and resistance—and work on developing each one with the information I give you in the following chapters.

ASSERTIVENESS

Assertiveness is the ability to exercise one's own rights without denying the rights of others. This builds upon *personal awareness, for a woman must first be in touch with what it is she wants or needs* in any given situation. Then comes the ability to express those needs and feelings honestly and comfortably and to stand up for them as necessary.

Assertiveness is one of the most effective techniques for preventing assault! For example, the assailant will often test a woman first, perhaps by coming very close to her or touching her to see how she will react. *An assertive response may prevent as much as 80 percent of potential assaults.*

Practicing assertiveness can have an immediate and profound effect on your daily life. Often, it take practice, just like anything else if it does not come immediately and easily to you.

Assertiveness is largely a learned behavior, and in our society men have traditionally been encouraged to practice it much more than women.

As women, we have often been trained to be caretakers and nurturers, responding to the needs of others before our own. We need to distinguish between the healthy exercise of caring—and its extreme—which can do violence to our sense of self. "Caretaking," which allows you to be attacked and injured, whether physically or emotionally, is actually inappropriate and can be perceived as *victim behavior,* particularly by those *who are perfectly aware that they are intruding on your rights.*

Permission to print granted by BAMM Impact, San Carlos, California.

CHAPTER THREE

Security in Your Home

MOST OF US know that we should lock our windows and doors, but you'd be surprised by how many people forget to lock them before leaving their houses or going to bed. Crime statistics show that one in four burglars enters through an unlocked door or window.

Now that you know that, it's time to take a look at your house from the outside. Pretend you're a thief who's casing the place. Walk around your house once during the day and once later in the evening, and really try to think like a criminal. Look for good hiding places to conceal yourself. If you can duck behind a large bush, hedge, or garbage can, that's not good. You shouldn't be able to do that.

So, when you're through casing, start cutting: Cut down any excessive foliage and remove any other barriers that a person could hide behind. Make sure all ladders and tools have been put away so that burglars can't use them. If possible, put your garbage cans in your garage. This not only keeps people from hiding behind them, but it keeps people from going through your garbage. You'd be surprised how much personal information can be found in household trash.

Now you're ready for the next test. When it's dark, close all your inside window coverings, including drapes, curtains, or blinds (if your garage has windows, make sure they are covered, too), and turn on your interior lights. Then go outside and see whether you can look into your house. If you can, purchase better window coverings. You don't want anyone watching you or your family.

Your Mailbox

Check your mailbox. It's best not to have your name on it. You should make sure that it has a locking device so that no one can look through your mail and figure out what your name is. Once someone has your name and address, he or she can easily get your phone number, call to see whether you're home, and rob you if you're not. I advise installing a covered mail slot in your front door with an interior hood so that a stranger can't peek into your house. Unfortunately, some local post offices don't allow this type of mail slot, so check with your postmaster before you make a change.

Perimeter Lighting

Ample exterior lighting is essential to your home security. Outside, photosensitive or solar energy lights, which go on at dusk and off at dawn, should be positioned on all exterior doors, bedroom windows, and even basement windows. Add automatic floodlights that use motion or heat sensors to detect a moving person. Before you buy them, however, make sure the detectors are equipped with a sensitivity switch, otherwise you'll have animals tripping the lights all night long.

These products are relatively inexpensive and can be purchased in hardware and home improvement stores.

Walls and Fences

Walls, fences, and security gates provide another layer of defense against intruders and make it more difficult for burglars to steal large objects. But even the highest wall can't stop someone who wants to get in.

Exterior Doors

Standard door locks will keep out the opportunist thief, but a more determined burglar can easily smash open a door with a well-placed kick. That's why it's a good idea to have metal-clad or solid hardwood doors that are secured with dead-bolt locks. To check the quality of wood on your present door, stick a push-pin into the door jam. If it goes in easily, the wood is soft, and I advise you to buy a new door.

However, when it comes to replacing your primary lock with a stronger one, it's far easier and better to add an auxiliary dead-bolt lock. Because of their superior pick and drill resistance, the best dead bolts are made by Medeco. If you already own a surface-mounted lock, you may be able to use a Medeco replacement cylinder, such as the Medeco 10W0400N. A Medeco lock lists for approximately $95 to $100. If you can't afford it, there are two other locks that I recommend: an Emhart's Kwikset dead bolt or double dead bolt or a Schlage dead bolt. Both cost under $45.

If you're wondering why a Medeco dead bolt costs more than a Schlage or Emhart one, here's the reason. The standard house key has five V-shaped cuts called *biting*, which coincide to pins of different heights inside the lock's cylinder. These locks are quite common and because their cylinders contain such a limited number of key configurations, it's actually possible for other keys to open *your* lock. Some lock cylinders have six pins instead of five, making such a fit less likely, but Medeco goes one step further, employing two different key configurations, which dictate different levels of protection. Medeco also offers a factory-only duplication option, which prevents any unwanted duplications.

When installing a lock, you'll also need to install a hinge, latch, and strike plate with screws that should be at least three inches long. Also, be aware that having windows on either side of a door is a security risk. My rule is that if you have a window within forty inches from a lock, you should consider removing the window and replacing it with something solid. For additional security, you may want to install steel screen doors fitted with heavy-duty hinges and cylinder locks.

Don't forget about your exterior garage doors. The last thing you want to have is someone break into your garage and wait there until you come home. To prevent garage break-ins, a standard overhead garage door should be secured with a hasp and padlock while an automatic garage door, which can be forced open by jerking it upward hard enough to break the cable or guide tracks, should be equipped with a special security device that sets off an alarm when someone tries to open the door from the outside without using the remote control. When you go on a trip, unplug the unit from its electrical socket.

Finally, install a wide-angle peep device in all exterior doors at a level where it can be used by all members of your family. If the disparity in heights is too great, install a second peephole or keep a footstool near the door.

I know it's a long list. Many of you, especially those of you who live alone, are probably asking yourselves, How am I going to make all these changes by myself? Well, I'm sure you know some of your neighbors and can find someone who can help you install your new security perimeter system. The important thing is, don't put it off, even if you are a renter and don't want to shell out the money to make improvements on a home you may soon leave.

If you are a renter, I suggest you talk with the owner of your house or the manager of your apartment building and discuss your concerns about security. Maybe the owner will make some monetary contribution toward upgrading the security of the dwelling. If he or she doesn't want to contribute, then you have no choice but to do it yourself. When it comes time to leave, try to negotiate some sort of compensation. If the owner or new tenant doesn't want to give you anything for what you've done, then take what's yours with you.

Windows

Now let's tackle your windows. It's important to understand that only metal bars or break-proof plastic like Mylar and Lexan, which is used in banks and some taxicab dividers, can keep a burglar out of your home. Glass breaks—that's a fact—and any burglar who's willing to risk making noise can get into your home. Personally, I don't like bars, because they create a fortress or prisonlike atmosphere, but if you decide on them, you should make sure they can be opened from the inside because you don't want to be trapped in your home if a fire breaks out. As far as glass goes, security expert Massad Ayoob recommends Globe Glass of Elk Grove, Illinois. It's a good, solid glass that can be purchased by most glaziers.

Now let's take a look at the lock on the window itself. Because burglars, robbers, and rapists prefer to work in silence, they'd rather break a lock than shatter a window. But don't rely on the type of window locks available at home improvement or hardware stores, because a burglar with a crowbar can easily rip these locks right off the sashes. I recommend that you drill through the window sashes and slip an eyebolt five-sixteenths

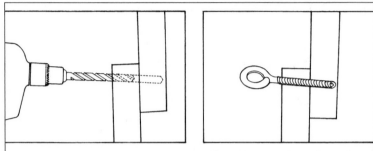

To secure windows shut, drill a hole through the sashes where they overlap, and insert a STRONG eyebolt to pin the sashes together. The only way to open the window is to remove the eyebolt.

of an inch in diameter into the hole you've made. The only drawback is that your windows will be permanently closed until you remove the eyebolt.

That isn't so bad if you have air-conditioning, but many women tell me that they don't have air-conditioning and can't keep their windows closed on warm nights. Others admit that they have air-conditioning but don't like to use it and prefer to sleep with their windows open. That may be okay if your bedroom is higher than the second floor and has no easy exterior access; you're probably fairly secure. However, if you're bedroom's on the first floor of either a home or apartment, you are not safe and need to purchase a window air conditioner. If you can't afford a new one, look for a used one or purchase a new one on a payment plan during the winter when prices are cheaper. When you install the air conditioner, make sure that it's bolted into the frame of the window so that it can't be pulled out.

Specialty Windows

- French windows, although elegant, are easy to force open. For added security, install sliding-bolt locks on the top and bottom at the window's center.

•If you have louvered window panes, consider replacing them. Louvered panes break easily and almost noiselessly when a screwdriver is inserted between them and gently pulled up. Replace them with casement windows that open and shut with a crank. If you can't replace the louvered windows with solid glass, then individual panes of glass can be securely fixed to the framework using epoxy glue. To keep the windows from being pried open, drill a hole through the movable mechanism and window frame, then insert a bolt or nail.

•Many of you may have sliding glass doors in your house. To immobilize the sliding panel, purchase a special steel or wood bar for $20 at your local hardware or home improvement store. If you don't want to permanently lock the sliding door, you can buy a special lock that's fitted for sliding glass doors, but beware, they can be compromised.

Interior Lighting

Here are the two basic rules when it comes to using your interior lighting for security purposes.

1. When you leave the house and return in the evening, you don't want to enter a darkened house.
2. If you go away on a trip, you want your house to look lived in while you're gone, with lights, radios, and televisions that switch on and off at various times.

There are different types of timers that you can buy, from a simple device that turns a single appliance (usually a light) on and off at prescribed times (approximately $15) to a more expensive and elaborate model, which can be programmed to control dozens of appliances (from $20 to $40). Whatever you

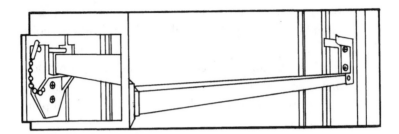

To keep the sliding panel of a door in place, purchase a steel or wood bar for about $20.

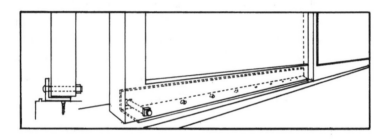

To keep the stationary half from being pulled out of the slide along the track, install a bracket made of angle iron. Use a piece about two-and- a-half-feet long with one-and-one-quarter-inch sides. Mark the bracket's position on the sill, then remove the door's retaining hardware and attach the bracket to the sill using three-inch flathead screws. Replace the door panel and attach the bracket to the door with a carriage bolt. You can also use an eyebolt to pin the two doors together, just as you would a double-hung window.

SOURCE: Consumer Reports, *February 1990.*

decide to buy, don't program the lights to go on or off at the hour or half-hour mark. We don't live that way. For example, program them to go on at six-thirteen P.M. and go off at eleven-eighteen P.M.

Home Security Systems

A home security system does two things for you. Not only is it a good deterrent to the criminal, but it acts as a warning device, allowing you the time and space you need to take action and initiate your home defense plan. However, don't count on it to save your and your family members' lives. That is your responsibility.

There are two types of alarm systems. One is installed by an alarm company and is patched into their security network or your local police department; the other, you install yourself and it's not connected to anything but your own home. If you decide to have an alarm company install a system, use one that is approved by the Underwriters' Laboratory and has been in operation for at least five years. Make certain it has a central alarm station that receives your alarm signal and promptly alerts the company's armed patrol or the local police to come to your assistance. Before purchasing an alarm system, check out the response time of the guards or police from other homeowners in the area. If it's more than six minutes, the perpetrator will have the time to do his work and leave.

Most home alarm systems transmit over phone lines. A professional burglar can easily cut the telephone wires leading into your home, so it's important to find out if your system will automatically sound an alarm if your telephone wires are cut. If not, make certain that a wireless transmitter is installed in your system, so if the wires are cut, the alarm will still be connected to your company's alarm station. If you already own a particular company's security system, check with them to see how the system functions when the line is severed. You may have to upgrade.

Besides installing door and window security sensors, it's also good to have motion detectors, especially in hallways and across large rooms. Ceiling-mounted smoke detectors should also be tied into your system.

I also recommend that you keep a panic button near your bed and carry a portable panic button on your key chain. Carry it while you're in the garage or walking up to your front door. It could be a real lifesaver. When most good alarm companies detect the panic alarm, they react quickly. If you don't answer the phone when they call you to check for a false alarm, the armed guards or police should come quickly to your house.

Every couple of months, check with your security system company to see if your security system's sensors and motion detectors are working properly. John J. Strauchs, a nationally recognized risk assessment and asset protection specialist, recommends that you think like a thief when testing motion sensors. Approach them from various angles and creep through the detection field below the minimum detection speed set by the company. If you have glass-break sensors, Strauchs suggests that you tap the glass with a screwdriver tip. If nothing happens, tap a little harder, but obviously, don't break the glass. Wait for the alarm to go off; it should still sound even if the glass isn't broken. If it doesn't, your sensors need to be adjusted.

Use the security system's yard signs and window stickers. In some cities, when homeowners installed an alarm system and put up the signs and stickers, attempted burglaries to their homes dropped by almost 100 percent.

You may want to have more than a detection system on the doors and windows of your home. You may also want to know when a car, truck, motorcycle, or even a bicycle is in your driveway. If you do want to go that far, there are now electromagnetic sensors that you can buy and bury underneath your driveway. Depending on the sensitivity level they are set to, they can detect the approach of something as big as a car or as small as a mouse and alert you to its presence by either sounding an alarm or activating an outdoor lighting system.

If you rent an apartment or don't want to purchase an expensive alarm system, there are number of good wireless do-it-yourself security system kits that include an instructional video and an 800 number to answer your questions. These wireless systems don't require you to drill holes or run wiring through your home, which means that when you move, you can take the system with you. Of course, none of these store-bought products can be hooked up to an alarm company or a police station.

High-Tech Home Automation for Security

There are a number of revolutionary electronic home automation wireless systems that can expand home security with or without a sophisticated security system. One of the best is the Mastervoice Intelligent Home Controller (IHC). The book-sized unit can control virtually every electric device in your house whether you're home or away. All you have to do is plug the IHC into any standard 110-volt outlet. Then attach any device you want to control—a lamp, television, air conditioner, patio light, driveway light, or even sprinkler system—to a X-10 powerhouse control module (available at electronic retailers).

This unbelievable little box has 99 timers that can control the power flow to up to 352 different devices. You can program a lamp to go on and off at certain times one day and totally different times another day. You can do special programming for weekends and even schedule your lights to go on and off according to the exact time of the daily sunrise or sunset, which the system keeps track of with a small database.

The IHC comes with one built-in motion sensor, and you can add up to sixteen others. The IHC is compatible with about 95 percent of the security systems currently being sold, which means you can use it with a system made and installed by a different company.

Finally, you can access the IHC at any time from a Touch-Tone phone. Whether you're in your house or in your car, a call can turn on or off any device in your home. This system starts at around $1,000, and for all it can do, I think that's a reasonable price.

The Safe Room in Your Home

Thirty-seven percent of rapes occur at night between the hours of six P.M. and six A.M., usually in a woman's bedroom. Even though you may have an alarm system, one of your best home defense strategies is to make your bedroom into a "safe room."

The first thing you need to do is install a solid-core door and equip it with a Medeco dead-bolt lock. Then purchase two flashlights along with extra bulbs and batteries and put them inside the room in a place where you can easily access them. Finally, you should keep a cellular phone by your bedside or install a second phone line that is not part of the regular house phone system.

Check if your bedroom has an escape route to the outside. Then ask yourself the following questions:

1. Can I get to a neighbor's house and ask for help?
2. Are my neighbors usually home?
3. If I need to run down an alley, is it safe?

If you live on the second floor without a fire escape, purchase a rope or chain ladder so you can leave through the window, and practice climbing down the ladder. Now, let's go over what you need to do if an intruder enters your house.

First, you'll retreat to your safe room (you might already be there), deadbolt the door, and call the police from your cellular phone or separate phone line. Then, when it becomes possible, leave the room through a window or door that takes you out-side. However, under no circumstances should you leave the safe room and look for the intruder in the house. *Remember*: Exiting the safe room could put you at a disadvantage. Wait for the police to arrive.

If you have children, everything changes a little. Instead of making your room into a safe room, it's better to make your youngest child's room into a safe room, because it saves time to bring everyone together in one child's room. When your children are mature enough and can understand the concept of home self defense, you may want them to create their own safe rooms and establish their own escape routes. For now, however, the most important thing is to rehearse responses to various scenarios that may occur. Also, teach your baby-sitters your safe room defense strategy.

If you have a large home, you may want to create a second safe room near your kitchen. Or if you use your den frequently, make that a safe room, too. Any room can be a safe room. I even know women who have made their bathrooms into safe rooms because they feel vulnerable while bathing.

If you live in a rental and can't afford to purchase a solid-core door and dead-bolt lock, you can improvise by buying a Door Jammer for approximately $29.95, which easily screws on to the bottom of your door. Once installed, all you have to do is push the Door Jammer's lever down with your foot, and the door can't be forced open unless someone literally breaks through it. I also recommend Door Jammers for your solid-core doors, including exterior doors.

A Portable Cellular Phone in Your Safe Room

Although an unlisted second phone line in your safe room is a good security measure, I prefer a portable cellular phone. Frequently, an intruder will cut the telephone wires, making it im-

The Door Jammer is an inexpensive and easy-to-install device that when activated stops an intruder from entering a room. It can be used on exterior doors as well as interior doors.

possible for you to call 911. If you have a portable cellular phone, you'll be able to make that call. These phones used to be rather pricey, but prices have come down, and you can keep your bills to a minimum by not giving your cellular number out to anyone (you get charged anytime someone calls you) and only using the phone in an emergency.

Telephone Answering Machines

More women are taking advantage of telephone answering machines not only for taking messages, but for screening unwanted calls. Because you don't want to convey any personal information to strangers, when you record your greeting, don't offer your name or phone number or say you're not at home. Also, don't use *I* in your greeting; use *we* to confuse the caller. If you're a woman living alone, you may want to have a man record the message. The best message is: "We can't get to the phone right now. Please leave your name, number, and a message, and we'll get right back to you as soon as possible. Thanks for calling."

Dealing with Nuisance or Threatening Phone Calls

While a telephone can be a lifesaver, it can easily become a mechanism of terror. Ask anybody who's received persistent, obscene phone calls from a stranger. It can be a very disturbing experience, shaking you to the core. "Why me?" you ask yourself. "Does he know me? Is he watching me when I'm outside? Will he come after me?"

However, there are ways to avoid getting such calls. If possible, don't list your name in the phone book. If you need to, only list your last name, and don't give a street address. Most single women use first initials; perverts know that and dial those numbers. (If you're a single man and want to help women, list yourself under your first initial and help confuse obscene callers.)

Another thing you can do is acquire a voice mail number so you won't be directly harassed at home, which I highly recommend to women living alone. Available in most cities, a voice mail number is a message service located in a neutral site, usually the offices of the company offering the service. In some cities, you can even subscribe to such a service through your local telephone company. It costs around $15 a month, and it's well worth it, because you can give this number out to anybody and not worry you are going to be harassed at home or at your office.

Along with the answering service, many phone companies have introduced two new features that can be added to your phone service for a nominal fee to prevent you from receiving obscene or annoyance calls. One is Call Block or Screen Call, and the other is Call Return.

Call Block stops any calls to your phone from a specific telephone number. When an obscene call is received, you punch in a code number, which signals the phone company's computer to trace the call and block any future calls that you receive from that number. After that, any time the obscene phone caller tries to call you, he or she will get a busy signal. If the phone caller switches to another phone, you can also block him or her from calling from that number as well.

The other feature, Call Return, requires your active participation. It works by recording the originating phone number and retaining it for a predetermined period of time. When you get an obscene phone call, hang up, then dial the Call Return code and you will be connected to the number that just called you. When the phone is answered, tell the caller not to make any more calls or you will report him or her to the phone company and the police. Most likely, the caller will never call you again, and if he or she does, just use the Call Block service.

Here are some other phone tips:

- When you receive a call that seems to be the wrong number, do not volunteer your phone number. If the caller requests it, ask what number he or she is trying to reach. Then verify their wrong number without mentioning your number.
- Be wary of telephone surveys. Don't participate in surveys that ask you anything personal or make you suggest that you are home alone.
- If your children answer the phone, instruct them to never give out any information. If you are not home, they should tell the caller that you can't come to the phone, but if he or she will leave their name and number, you'll call them later. Keep emergency phone numbers handy for your children, and consider telephone security a part of your home security plan. Setting up obstacles on all fronts makes you and your family less of a target.

Dogs

If you don't have a dog, give serious consideration to owning one. Studies indicate that homes with dogs are less likely to be burglarized than homes without them.

There are three different categories of dogs: a watchdog, a protection-trained dog, and an attack dog. A watchdog requires less training, and size doesn't matter. It can be big or small, it just has to bark when someone comes near your house, alerting you that you have a visitor, wanted or unwanted. The dog's bark also lets the visitor know that he or she has been detected.

One of the easiest ways to train a watchdog is to chain it to a tree when it's about six months of age. If possible, ask a stranger to invade the dog's territory and run away. When the dog reacts, praise him excessively. Do this drill a few times a day for a week, and soon your dog will know to bark when a stranger comes near your house, yard, or car.

For some people, having this simple warning is good enough, but others prefer a protection-trained dog, which has advanced obedience training. On your command, it barks and lunges at an aggressor without actually biting him or her. Also, on your command, it immediately sits and is silent. The training is oriented strictly toward a deterrent show of force, although if the

A Schutzhund trainer uses a heavily padded sleeve and work pants when training a dog to do "bite work." The stick is beaten on the sleeve to help excite the dog. It is not used on the dog.

attacker persists, the animal may fall back on its natural protective instinct and bite.

Don't expect a small dog to be an effective protection dog since they are not very intimidating and can be warded off with a strong kick. You want a dog that weighs at least fifty pounds. I recommend buying a Doberman, Rottweiler, German shepherd, Great Dane, Akita, or Rhodesian Ridgeback from a reputable breeder. None of these dogs come cheap. Expect to spend between $500 and $5,000. If you can't afford these prices, large mixed breeds are just as good and many are more emotionally more stable than the larger registered dogs.

There are many good dog trainers, but one of the best programs is provided by an organization called Schutzhund, which was begun in Germany and has chapters worldwide. If you request it, a trainer at Schutzhund will teach your dog to attack on command, but I don't recommend turning your dog into an attack dog, because he will become unsuitable for the average household. On his master's command or when he sees his master being assaulted, an attack dog will sink his teeth into a person. He is supposed to stop biting once an attacker stops resisting, but the only problem is, sometimes he doesn't. For that reason, this type of dog cannot be allowed to run free. One bite too many may cost someone, especially a child, his or her life, and you will undoubtedly be sued for thousands, if not millions, of dollars.

The benefits of owning a dog far outweigh the risks. For instance, if you take your dog with you in your car, there's much less of a chance you'll be carjacked. When you walk around with a large dog, the likelihood of you being attacked is greatly reduced. That's why I recommend that real estate agents, traveling saleswomen, and women who work in unsafe areas take their trained dogs with them.

In the course of my work, I've come across a unique nonprofit organization in Eugene, Oregon, called Project Safe Run, which shows what a good security tool a dog can be. Founded in 1981 by Shelley Reecher, Project Safe Run provides trained dogs to women on a monthly basis for a small donation of $25. Meanwhile, senior citizens, women or men, may use the dogs free of charge.

The dogs may be used only for running, jogging, or walking purposes. A woman may reserve a dog day or night, seven days a week, and she is matched with a protection dog that enables her to walk or run safely at her own pace. The women come from college campuses, athletic clubs, apartment complexes, private homes, and retirement centers.

Each dog undergoes rigorous training, including simulated assaults, and when he is accompanying a woman, the dog works on a six-foot leash and wears a little backpack that can hold money, keys, and other personal items. Beforehand, the women are informed of the commands for obedience and watch-alert, and they are told how to prevent involvement with other animals and protect children who might want to pet the dog.

If threatened by an assailant, the dog positions itself in front of the woman and gives warning by barking, growling, and bearing his teeth. The dog is trained to protect, not attack, and so he matches the level of aggression with that of the assailant. Only if the attacker continues to approach will the dog bite, but never will he turn on the person he is protecting, because he only responds to threatening moves and not coded attack commands.

The effectiveness of Project Safe Run's training format is documented by their 9,000 safe runs without a single accidental bite or assault. Its founder is starting other nonprofit voluntary groups in other parts of the country.

Teaching Your Children Home Security

When you think your children are mature enough to learn about security in the home, begin giving them some basic pointers, but try not to scare them. Talk about strangers. Ask them to tell you who a stranger is. Tell them *never* to open a door to a stranger even if you or your husband is home. If they do talk to a stranger through a door, they should be instructed to say "My mother and father can't come to the door right now," even if neither of you are home. The children should then alert their caregiver that someone is at the door.

Teach them about closing windows and doors. If you have a home security system, instruct them in its usage. Once you've decided which rooms are your safe rooms, run through a drill of retreating to the primary safe room if someone breaks into the house. When your children are mature enough, they can have their own bedrooms be their safe rooms, and they can lock their dead bolt every night, although you should have a key to open it in case of an emergency. (In fact, all the dead-bolt locks should open with the same key.)

It's also a good idea to teach them about phone security. For example, they should never say they are alone or tell a stranger who calls where *you* might be.

Marking and Recording Your Property

Although it takes time, I recommend that you take a weekend off to identify and record your personal property. Use an inexpensive engraving pen to engrave cameras, televisions, VCRs, stereos, and so on with your driver's license number preceded by the first two letters of your state. (For example, if you're a

California resident begin with the letters *CA*.) Items that can't be marked, such as paintings and jewelry, should be photographed with your driver's license number included in the picture. If you don't have a driver's license, use your social security number. When items are marked, it's more difficult for burglars to sell them. If they're found after being stolen, you'll get them back quicker from the police.

Neighborhood Watch Programs

If your neighborhood or block doesn't have a Neighborhood Watch program, talk to your neighbors about forming a network to watch for and report suspicious people and their activities to the police. To get the program started, contact your local police station. After it's organized, it's important to go the meetings to find out what's happening in your area and how you can continue to participate. Neighborhood Watch programs work.

The more personally secure you are, the more you feel good about who you are and your connections to other people and your roots in a community, the more you are able to change.

—President Bill Clinton, speech on crime given in August 1993, from *The New Republic,* October 18, 1993, p. 12.

Home Self-Defense Strategies

Once you've made your home as impenetrable as possible from criminal intrusion, it's hard to imagine what you would do if someone successfully broke into your home while you were there. But no matter how many precautions you take or how many security devices you install, there still remains the possibility, however small, of someone getting into your home. Therefore, it's imperative that you have a clear understanding of what you will do in the event that this happens.

Let's start with a scenario: It's ten forty-five on a Thursday night. You're in your bathroom, wearing an oversized T-shirt and sneakers. You've just finished brushing your teeth, and as you turn off the faucet, you hear a window break in a downstairs room. You turn your head and listen more carefully and hear creaking footsteps, which you know are coming from the kitchen because of the sound they make as they cross the tiles. You realize someone's in your house and you're scared.

What will you do next? Do you know? Do you have a home defense plan? Hopefully, you do by now, but for this scenario, let's use mine. I'd race to my bedroom, which is my safe room, shut the solid-core door, bolt the dead-bolt lock, call 911 on my portable cellular phone, and then exit through my second-floor window, using a rope ladder that I have stored under my bed. I'd do all that within three minutes. No problem.

But now let's complicate things a bit. Let's say your husband is out of town and you're with your five-year-old daughter and nine-year-old son when someone breaks in.

Here's what I'd do: I'd rush down the hallway, pull my son out of his bed, and run with him to my daughter's room, which is my family's primary safe room. I'd close the solid-core door, lock the dead bolt, then call 911 from a second telephone line. I'd tell the police operator that my children and I are barricaded in the southeastern corner bedroom and that, when they arrive, I'll throw the front door keys down to them. For just such an occasion, I have an extra set of keys stored in a small yellow box in my daughter's room. (I have the keys in a yellow box so that they will be easily seen in the dark.) All this can be

done in three minutes or less if you practice.
Take the time to think about what you would do if a criminal breaks into your home. If you live with other people, discuss and practice various strategies. If you have a protected perimeter, a security system, and a plan of action to follow, you will not live in a state of fear.

CHAPTER FOUR

Security in Your Car

MANY AMERICANS SPEND as many as two hours a day driving a car, and most of them feel relatively safe doing it. But it turns out a car is one of the least safe places to be. From the 18 million accidents or so that occur each year, there are almost 50,000 auto fatalities.

If that isn't enough, we now have a new hazard to deal with—carjacking, the fastest growing American crime. With so many cars having antitheft devices installed in them, thieves have decided it's easier to hold you up either while you're in your car or near it, take your keys, and then drive off with your vehicle. Even though carjacking is a federal crime with a mandatory fifteen-year sentence (if the victim is killed the law mandates a life sentence), most carjackers are never caught. Actual statistics aren't known, but it's been estimated that there were more than 23,000 carjackings in 1993.

Carjacking is a quick crime, usually taking no longer than fifteen seconds and may occur anywhere you stop your car: At stop signs, traffic lights, intersections, parking lots, gas stations, and even private driveways. Women are more vulnerable than men. Even couples are at risk. Those of you who live in small towns are vulnerable, too, because carjacking is spreading to rural highways.

For some gang members, carjacking is part of their initiation rights. However, most car thieves want your car for parts they can sell on the U.S. black market. For this reason, they target specific makes and models, and because so much money is at stake, many carjackers are willing to kill you to get what they need.

What to Do If You're Carjacked

If you are carjacked and the carjacker has a weapon, don't fight back. Give the attacker your keys. If he wants your purse, give it to him, too. Just hope that's all he wants.

If he tries to force you into your car, one of the best suggestions I've heard comes from self-defense experts Craig Fox Huber and Don Paul. They recommend fainting or going limp and becoming deadweight. But if you feel that the attacker is going to kill you, then you might as well fight.

On the other hand, if you're already in the car, and the carjacker has a gun or knife pointed at your throat and growls "Start driving, bitch," start driving and when you feel the time is right—and only you can judge when—crash into another car. You have to hope that he'll panic and jump out of the car and won't try to kill you. But the last thing you want is to end up with him in a deserted area, where your chances of survival are very poor.

Immediate Precautions

These are some precautions you can take against carjacking. Some of these suggestions will set up barriers, making it more difficult for criminals to target you and your car. Other advice will help you to quickly report a carjacking.

- Keep your car keys separate from your house keys.
- Use a post office box mailing address on your auto registration.
- Memorize your car's license plate number.
- Tint your side windows and keep them clean. When opening your car door, you can use them as mirrors to keep an eye out for anybody approaching you from behind. The other advantage to having tinted windows is that they make it more difficult for a carjacker to look in your car and see who's there. If he can't tell who's inside, he's less likely to attack.
- If you have electric car doors, purchase a remote door opener that you can keep on your key chain. Make sure that the opener only opens the driver's door.
- This may sound extreme, but law enforcement officials have told me it's a good idea to keep a man's tie and jacket in the backseat of your car, because some carjackers target women owners based on the objects they see inside their cars. Once they think they've found a car that belongs to a woman, they will then hide out and wait until she returns to her car.
- Consider buying a dog. While driving around town or traveling on the road, a big dog, like a German shepherd or a Rottweiler, is a great deterrent against carjacking.
- Keep your car windows and doors locked at all times. If you don't have air-conditioning, keep the driver's window slightly open and close it when you stop at intersections.
- Join LoJack if your local police utilizes this system for locating and recovering stolen cars.

Parking Lots

You are most vulnerable to an attack, whether it be a carjack-ing, robbery, or rape, during the few seconds you are getting into or out of your car. As a result, a parking lot, especially at night, is one of the most likely settings for a crime to take place. It stands to reason, then, that you should try to heighten your awareness when parking or returning to your car. The first thing to consider is where you should park. I suggest parking as close to the entrance of the lot as possible, or if the facility has valet parking, consider using this service. Often, I drive around a parking lot for more than five minutes before finding a good space. While driving around, I look out for suspicious persons. If I feel uncomfortable, I leave the area. However, once I find a good space, I back into it, because later, if I have to drive away in a hurry, I know it will be much easier to drive out of the space forward than backward. Then I gather together the things I want to take with me and check one last time for ques-tionable people. Only then do I open the door and proceed on my way.

When you leave a shopping mall, supermarket, office build-ing, restaurant, or other public facility, stop for a moment be-fore entering the parking area. Assess the situation. Look around. If you see anyone suspicious, go back inside and tell the manager or a security guard of your concerns and request that someone accompany you to your car.

Carry your keys as you walk to and from your car. If you have a pepper spray canister, have it in the ready position. From a distance, take a quick look underneath your car to see whether someone is lying there. Believe it or not, carjackers use this method to initiate a surprise attack. They wait under your car until you come back, then grab you by the ankles and pull you down to the pavement. You should also look in one of the back windows before opening any of your car doors. Make sure that no one is hiding on the floor, even if the car was valet-parked.

Be especially aware of your surroundings while you're opening and closing the car door. As soon as you're in, lock the door, start up the motor, and move out of your space. Put your seat belt on last.

If you're outside the car and someone is approaching you, get inside and lock the door, even if it means leaving your packages. If the attacker doesn't have a weapon, lean on the horn. Start the car and get going. If you feel your life is in danger, use your car as a weapon against the attacker. You may have to hit him to stop him from attacking you.

Often, women think they are safer with children, but today's criminal has no respect for human beings and doesn't seem to care who he (and sometimes she) attacks. If your child or children need to be placed in car seats in the back of the car, you should get in the back of the car with them. Why? Because if you have to stand outside the car to help them get in their seats, you leave yourself open to danger, especially if you have your back turned and are concentrating on your children. This way, you can immediately get in the car and lock the doors. Then, after you've strapped your children in, climb up into the driver's seat.

If you have your hands full with grocery or shopping bags, you may want to have someone from the store put the bags in the trunk while you're strapping the kids into their seats.

Follow-Home Carjacking

Frequently, carjackers work in pairs and follow you home. They may have watched you leave a restaurant, supermarket, bank, gas station, or your place of work. Later, as you turn into your driveway or park in front of your house, one of them, usually

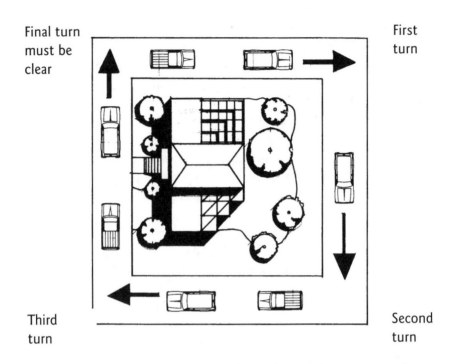

The rule of four turns: If you think someone is following you, make four right turns. If the same car is behind you when you come back out to your original route, drive to a busy gas station, a restaurant, or a police station. SOURCE: *Secure from Crime by Craig Fox Huber and Don Paul (Woodland, Calif.: Path Finder Publications, 1994).*

the passenger, will jump out of *his* car and the next thing you know you'll have a gun pointed at your head. Most simply say "Get out and leave the keys." Others add that if you do as you are told, nothing will happen to you. Most of the time that's true, but occasionally it isn't, so consider yourself lucky if he just pulls you out of your car and drives away. Sounds humiliating, even frustrating? Well, it is, but there isn't much you can do once the act has begun. However, there are some preventive measures you can take.

First, as you drive home, always check in your rearview mirror to see who's behind you. Take note of the make and model of the car and check to see who's inside. If it's dark, and you have trouble identifying either the car or the occupants, take note of the headlight configuration and scrutinize the silhouette of the driver and passengers, checking for head heights, hats, and hairstyles. Don't be fooled if you see a man and a woman or two women.

When a person (or persons) is following you and sees that you're looking back at him and "marking" him, he realizes you know he's following you. In many instances, he'll abort his attack and find another target since the element of surprise is gone. (*Remember:* A criminal's success often depends on surprise.) Of course, you'll never know whether he was really following you, but there is an easy way to check. If you feel you are being followed, make four right turns. If the same car is behind you when you come back to your original route, don't go home. Drive to a restaurant, a busy gas station, a fire station, or to the police station and report that you're being followed, even though the car has probably left you by then and moved on to another target.

Intersections, Stops, and Signal Lights

Many carjackings occur at traffic signals, where drivers become complacent while waiting for the light to change. Some of you may shift into neutral and use the time to apply makeup, put on nail polish, or read your mail or a newspaper. But this is the time to be alert.

Remember to:

•Make it a habit to leave ample room between you and the car ahead of you, so that, if you have to, you can make a quick turn into the next lane and accelerate quickly.

- Try to stay in the middle lane when coming to a stop (unless you have to make a right turn). If you stop in a lane nearer to the curb, it gives an attacker easier access to your car.
- Just say no if someone comes up to your car and wants to wash your windshield. If he persists, start your windshield wiper, spritz your washer fluid, and lean on your horn.
- Go through the intersection if anyone approaches your car and you feel in danger, even if the light is red. (Try to wait until there's no traffic.) I'd rather risk getting a traffic ticket than losing my life.

Traffic Accidents

Frequently, carjackers will bump into the back of a car to get the driver to pull over and get out of his or her car. If this happens to you and you feel threatened by the driver who has hit you, don't get out of your car. Suggest driving to a public place, like a gas station. If the other driver insists that you get out of your car, lean on the horn or drive away. If you get hit in an isolated area and it doesn't seem like an accident, continue driving and get away from your pursuer.

On the other hand, if the driver of the other car approaches you with a weapon and you don't feel you can get away in time, give up the car immediately. Get out. Don't take anything, and don't look him straight in the eye because he could become anxious if he thinks you will be able to identify him later on. Don't talk to him. If you have children in the car, say loudly, with your eyes averted, "There's a child in the back of the car." Then get your son or daughter out of the car and leave.

Try not to be paranoid. Most accidents are legitimate, and you can exchange information. But even then, you must be careful. Never give out your home address or phone number, except to the police. Joe Poyer, the editor of *Safe & Secure Living* magazine, says you should "give the other driver only your driver's license number and the name, address, and telephone number of your insurance agent. If you don't have an agent, then only provide your work address or your work number."

Highway Driving

If you travel on highways on a regular basis, here are some tips:

•When another driver gestures to you that something is wrong with your car, don't pull over to the side of the road immediately, because it may be a trick to lure you off the highway. Keep on driving, and if the radio is on, turn it off. Listen to your car and try to determine if there's anything wrong. If you don't hear anything out of the ordinary or see smoke, the supposed problem can wait until you get to the next available gas station. But as you continue to drive, watch out for the other car. If the driver starts to harass you by following you too closely, take the car's license plate number, and get off the highway when you see a well-populated area. Then drive to a restaurant or gas station and call the police.

•This may seem obvious, but don't pick up hitchhikers—even a female hitchhiker. Although you may want to help a woman stranded on the side of the road next to her car, don't stop. She could be a decoy. The best thing you can do is call 911 from your cellular phone if you have one; otherwise use a pay phone at the nearest gas station and give the police a description of the woman and tell them where you saw her.

Stranded on the Highway

There are a couple of precautions you can take to avoid becoming stranded on the highway. The most obvious is to keep your gas tank at least half full at all times. The other is to make sure you take your car in for regular inspections and tune-ups. Other than that, there's little else you can do, so let's concentrate on what you should do if you find yourself in this predicament.

First, make sure you pull your car safely off the road and put your hazard signal on. This becomes particularly important at night, when you are most in danger of getting hit by an approaching car. If you think you are in danger of being hit, then get out of your car immediately and stand away from it. But if not, it's best to stay in your car and assess your surroundings. Obviously, if you have a cellular phone, call 911 and tell the police dispatcher where you are. However, don't say that you're alone, because you don't know who might be listening to your conversation and try to take advantage of the situation. As you know, calls from cellular phones often "cross lines," so I suggest you say "My husband and I are . . ."

Whether you have a phone or not, the next thing you should do is take a look around. If you are in an area where there are trees and bushes, you may be more secure hiding behind one of them until the police arrive. (Even if you don't call, a highway patrol car will eventually pass by and spot your car.) By taking cover, you not only avoid making yourself a target but you have a leg up on anyone who approaches your car.

Motor Vehicle Thefts

According to the 1991 FBI Uniform Crime Report:

- One out of every one hundred seventeen vehicles is stolen.
- A vehicle is stolen every nineteen seconds.
- A vehicle, or its contents or accessories, is stolen every seven seconds.
- Approximately 4,550 cars will be stolen today.
- Law enforcement agencies cleared only 13.3 percent of the motor vehicle theft in 1991.

Auto Air Bag Thefts

Car burglars are stealing air bags from cars parked in parking lots, driveways, and auto dealerships throughout the country, especially on the East and West Coasts. The safety devices, which can cost up to $1,200, are then sold to unscrupulous body shop operators and mechanics who want the bags at reduced rates to install in cars involved in accidents in which the factory-installed bag inflated. According to auto insurance sources, a body shop with a supply of stolen air bags can pocket the difference between what is paid to the thief and the $1,000 or more that is billed to an insurance company or car owner for a new bag.

Antitheft Devices

Every year, people spend millions of dollars attempting to make their cars burglarproof. One of the simplest and least expensive mechanisms is the Club, a steering wheel locking device that you've probably seen advertised on TV. It's somewhat effective but mostly as a deterrent, because if a thief has the right tools and the desire, he can remove the Club by either drilling a hole in its lock or sawing it off with a hacksaw. Other inexpensive devices are engine-kill switches and fuel shutoff mechanisms that prevent a thief from driving very far, but these, too, can be compromised by professionals.

Currently, there are more than fifty different types of car alarms that can be installed in your car, ranging in price from $50 to $700. For example, a recent article in the *New York Times* talked about a new device made by Malvy Technology of Oklahoma City, which is "designed to deter auto theft by causing the steering wheel to spin impotently when the owner removes the key. Car thieves who hot-wired the automobile would drive away at their peril because there would be no way to steer the vehicle." The only drawback of the device, which costs between $600 and $700, is that there is a high probability that the thief will end up crashing your car, maybe even totaling it.

Are car alarms effective? Are they a deterrent against vehicle theft? Unfortunately, there's no real answer because if a car thief wants your car, he'll steal it no matter how elaborate an alarm system you own. In the same *New York Times* article that describes the Malvy device, Charles Hurley, a spokesman for the Insurance Institute for Highway Safety, says that "most auto-theft devices are easily defeated by professional thieves." But, at the same time, I've had friends who have seen novices dart away from a car when the alarm goes off. So you never know. It's probably better to have one than not to have one, but before you install anything, you should contact your insurance company to find out whether they offer a premium discount if you install a particular type of alarm. Sometimes companies only approve devices approved by the Underwriters' Laboratory.

Armored Cars

With violent crime as high as it is in the United States, more and more professionals and celebrities are purchasing armored cars. For a couple of hundred thousand dollars you can pick one up, too, or have your present vehicle fitted with a bulletproof suit for around $100,000. Some suits are heavier than others and stop higher-caliber bullets, but new improvements in technology, design, and construction have made armored cars virtually indistinguishable from normal cars.

Because armor adds weight to a car, it can decrease the auto's acceleration and maneuverability, so you should test-drive several cars before deciding on one. All doors and windows and the rear of the passenger seats and gas tank should be fortified. Different types of materials are available for this, including Kevlar, ceramic, and dual hard steel. Safoam, a plastic spongelike material, can be installed inside the gas tank and help prevent an explosion if the tank is punctured by gunfire. Protective windows are extremely important, but remember that even the strongest bullet-resistant glass is not bulletproof.

There are only a few armored vehicle manufacturers in the country, and you probably won't find them in the Yellow Pages. I suggest contacting your local police department or a nearby car manufacturer. They will probably be able to tell you where you can find one.

SOURCE: *Anthony Scotti, Executive Safety & International Terrorism.*

The Best Cars for Women to Own

When women buy cars, few of them think in terms of defense. Once you become security savvy, however, all that changes. Before you go shopping for a car, the first thing you should do is contact your local police department to find out what the three most popular stolen vehicles are in your area. That may rule out certain makes. If you're considering a convertible, you should think about the hazards of driving in an open car, especially when you're stopped at an intersection, where you'll be a sitting duck for a carjacker who can be in your car in seconds.

You should also think about whether you need a two-door or a four-door car. If you don't have children, you should probably opt for a two-door, because it leaves you with fewer locks to keep track of. You should also get a car with power windows and doors, but set the system so that when you unlock the driver's door, the others won't unlock, too. If they all open at once, a carjacker can easily slide in on the passenger side.

All these things aside, do I think there are certain cars that are safer for women than others? Yes, I do, most notably utility trucks, which include the Jeep Cherokee, Ford Explorer, and Chevy Suburban, among others. First, a utility truck is higher off the ground than conventional cars, so you can survey the terrain around you better when you drive, especially in traffic. It also keeps people who are in "shorter" cars from seeing into yours, which makes you less vulnerable to attack. Finally, a utility truck has a strong, independent, sporty image, which transfers onto its woman owner, who, as a result, feels and looks more confident when she's driving.

So next time you purchase a car, think not only about colors and accessories, but your own security.

Evasive Driving Courses

If you really want to be a smart driver and have the time and money, I suggest you take an evasive driving course. A couple of years ago, I took one at Executive Security International (ESI) in Aspen, Colorado, and I had a blast. Not only did I learn how to get away from trouble on the road, but I had a wild time doing 180-degree bootlegger turns and ramming other cars in a beat-up Dodge with a helmet on. I recommend ESI's program, Bob Bondurant's course in California, or Anthony Scotti's class in Massachusetts (see the appendix).

The height disparity between the sporty Jeep Cherokee and the classic BMW.

CHAPTER FIVE

Security in Offices and Other Public Places

DESPITE THE PRESENCE of security guards, you aren't as safe as you might think in office buildings and other public facilities. Unfortunately, only a few states have laws that regulate the screening procedures for hiring security guards, so some of them may actually have criminal records. That's why it's important to get to know the guards in your building and to watch out for guards you don't recognize. If a new guard comes on duty, ask a guard you know to introduce you.

It's also good to have a rapport with the guards in case you have to work late. When you work after hours, you may want to tell one of the guards at the front desk that you'll be in your office until a specific time and ask him to check on you if you don't leave the building shortly after that time. Also, ask him to call you if he hears that there's a suspicious person in the building.

Elevators

Elevators are the most unsafe areas in public buildings, especially after hours, when few people are around. A mugger can quickly take control of the situation by flipping the emergency stop button in between floors.

In fact, at one time or another, you may have felt apprehensive while standing in an elevator with a strange man, waiting to arrive at your floor. Your heart starts to beat harder, and you just can't wait to have those doors open and get out as quickly as possible. For most of us, this is a normal reaction, because in our culture, it isn't natural for strangers to be thrown together in such close quarters for even a short period of time. But for others, especially those who have been attacked in an elevator, this fear may be more pronounced and may even lead to the development of a phobia.

"After the attack," one of my students said, "whenever I was alone with a man in an elevator, my heart would start racing and I'd experience shortness of breath."

It had started early one Friday evening, when most people had already gone home, when she returned to her downtown Los Angeles office building to pick up some documents. She said hello to the security guard at the front desk, then got in the elevator and pushed the button for the thirty-first floor. However, the elevator stopped at the third floor and a man in his late thirties got on. He was wearing a business suit and carrying a briefcase. "He looked like someone who would be working in the building, so I didn't get that nervous," she said, "I was a little uncomfortable, but I wasn't paranoid or anything." She moved to the back of the elevator and watched him push the button for the eighteenth floor. Then, to calm her nerves, she opened her appointment book and checked her schedule for the upcoming week.

A few floors went by—she heard the beeping sound—then, the next thing she knew, the elevator had stopped in between floors and the man had turned around and was pointing a knife at her. "Give me your purse and shut up or I'll kill you." She handed him her purse. He took it with his left hand, then punched her in the face with his right, knocking her out momentarily. A few seconds later, she woke up on the floor of the elevator. They were going down, and in a fog, she watched the man get out on the sixth floor and quickly walk away. Dazed by the blow and the confrontation, she lay on the floor of the elevator for nearly a minute before she got up and pushed the lobby button.

Could she have avoided being attacked? I think she probably could have.

The first thing she could have done was not return to the office after hours, when the building was almost deserted. Rule number 1 is to try to coordinate your work schedule with at least one other person's schedule, so that you can come and go together.

Rule number 2 is if you feel uncomfortable, don't enter an elevator with anybody you don't know. If you only have to travel a few floors, consider taking the stairs. At least you can run away from an attacker in a stairwell. As soon as the man got on the elevator my student could have gotten off and walked away purposefully, then come back and waited for another elevator.

She had said she really wasn't that nervous, even though it was after hours, because she'd done it dozens of times before and never had a problem. So, in that case, instead of retreating to the back of the elevator, she should have immediately moved to the front, next to the elevator button panel, and literally guarded the emergency stop switch. I also told her that she shouldn't have opened her appointment book and started reading it. Instead, she should have been keeping an eye on the man, especially his hands. That way, if she felt uncomfortable, she could have pressed a lower floor button and gotten off.

Don't think that just because you're in a crowded elevator you're safe from crime either. You'd be surprised how deftly thieves work in crowded elevators. So hold your purse tightly against your body.

Public Rest Rooms

The second most dangerous place in a public area is the rest room, especially ones in subway stations, highway rest stops, and shopping malls.

In general, it's better to use a bathroom that you need a key to enter. Many offices and gas stations have taken this precaution, although it doesn't automatically make the bathroom safe. If it's a single-person rest-room, you should lock the entrance door, then take a quick peek under the toilet stall door to see if anyone is actually using the toilet. If you hear a suspicious noise and are afraid someone might be hiding in the stall, you may want to push the door open strongly and stand back until you see that the stall is empty.

Larger public bathrooms can be dangerous, too, especially if they are empty. The same rules apply here. Check the stalls and keep your ears open. Also, when you use the toilet, it's a good idea to hold your purse rather than put it on the floor or hang it on a door hook. If someone enters the rest-room, become aware of their presence, but don't panic. Millions of people work in public buildings, and in most instances, whether you're in an elevator or a rest-room, you are relatively secure, especially if you remain alert and act in a prudent manner.

Security in the Workplace

Unfortunately, even your office, large or small, can be unsafe. I've heard stories of women having their checks stolen, purses ripped off, and valuable documents lifted from their offices, so here are some tips on office security:

• Report any strangers in your office to the office manager or to a security guard, preferably the one in charge. People hide in offices and steal after hours.

- Be wary of solicitors, including teenagers selling boxes of candy for a good cause. They should have ID's, but be aware that their ID's may be fake.

- Don't prop open office doors after hours. Keep all perimeter doors locked. If someone knocks on the office's main entrance door after hours, don't open the door until you've verified who the person is.

- Never leave your checkbook at work. Someone may go through your drawers and may steal a couple of your checks. If they're smart, they'll take the checks from the middle of the book, leaving the top ones in place. That way, you'll only notice the missing checks days or weeks later.

- Keep your purse near you at all times or lock it in a drawer or closet.

- If you're in charge of hiring new employees, wait until you've given them a trial period of three months before giving him or her a key to your office or the combination to a safe. Know your employees!

- If you make regular bank deposits, don't leave the office at the same time every day or use the same route. Avoid being predictable.

- Check out the layout of your office. Plan an escape route in case of an emergency.

- If a construction company or other type of company is doing work in your office, be aware of what they are doing. If possible, know the workers' names and the number of people working on the job.

- If you work in a cubicle area or open area, try to position yourself so you can see the entrance to the office area. That way you can watch the comings and goings of people.

Destroying Valuable Papers or Information

Any paper you throw out can be retrieved by a trash-can thug. Obviously, you might take more care in disposing of important office memos and business letters, but some documents that may appear harmless in fact contain plenty of valuable information. Think about all the preapproved credit card applications you toss out. And don't forget about all the receipts that end up in the garbage: the credit card charge slips, phone bills, duplicate physician bills, and bank statements. If these got into a criminal's hands, you might soon discover you have a serious problem.

There is, however, a simple precaution you can take. Shred all your documents, using a paper shredder, which you can purchase for under $50. The less expensive models shred paper into thin strips, which is fine, but they can only shred a limited number of pages at one time. The best models, like the ones some government agencies have, can turn hundreds of pages of paper into confetti in a matter of seconds.

The alternatives to using a machine won't win you any points with environmentalists, but you can tear up your important papers and flush the pieces down the toilet or burn them in your fireplace if you have one. In comparison, these methods of destruction may be a bit crude, but they are just as effective.

Domestic Violence

Domestic violence is endemic throughout the world, but it is the least reported, seldom punished crime. In the United States, it is publicly discussed and in the last few years, all fifty states and the District of Columbia have legislated civil-protection laws or injunctions that can be issued against an abusive spouse or lover. Many states also have laws against repeated violence that protect victims who don't live with, and/or are not related to, their abusers. These laws protect both women and men, but over 95 percent of physical abuse is committed by men against women.

It occurs in all religions, races, and socio-economic groups. Once a woman is battered, her chances of being battered again is high. A study conducted by the Kansas City Police Department finds that in 85 percent of the domestic-homicide incidents, the police were called to the house at least once in the preceding two years; in half of the incidents, police were called five times or more.

The statistics are astounding:

- Every fifteen seconds in the United States, a woman is beaten by her partner.
- In 1993, 1 million women required medical attention for injuries caused by battering.
- Every day, ten women die in the United States due to domestic violence.

Dr. Judy K. Wilson and John A. Shook of Creative Services, Inc., a rape crises–spouse abuse center in Marion County, Florida, describe in *Women's Self Defense* magazine the escalating pattern of domestic violence: "Physical violence between partners often happens for the first time after the third month of marriage or during the first pregnancy. Abusive partners use physical violence because it works to control the victim in a short time. He then uses apology and affection followed by more violence to 'condition' his victim. And, before long the 'hostage syndrome' sets in . . . The batterer slowly and deliberately isolates his partner. She becomes totally dependent upon him for every aspect of her life. He controls their money. He separates her from all of her friends and family, and requires his permission for any of their activities. He insidiously trains her as one would an animal, using fear, violence and intimidation, mixed with rewards and devoted affection."

Wilson, who has worked with hundreds of spouse-abuse families over the last thirty years, says that if a man has slapped his wife once or twice and then stopped, the marriage has a chance to survive. But, if the the violence continues beyond that point, Wilson contends that the violence cycle has begun and probably will never change, only escalate. Law enforcement officials estimate that 29 percent of female homicide-victims are killed by a husband or lover—most often when they are attempting to leave the relationship.

Domestic Violence in the Workplace

Often, current and former husbands and boyfriends commit more than 13,000 acts of violence against women in the workplace every year, according to estimates in a July, 1994 U.S. Justice Department report.

Many employers do little to protect or counsel victims, and often they will terminate the woman if they feel other workers are in danger. However, other employers offer assistance programs and some companies' security staff and receptionists will be alerted to keep the abuser away from the workplace.

Some employers will even allow the victim to alter her work schedule to make her life less predictable. Others will give women time off for court hearings and to file police complaints without losing vacation or sick days.

What Can You Do If You're Physically Abused?

If you are in an abusive relationship, I suggest that you begin to take steps to leave your partner. This is not easy to do. You may love him. You may not be economically independent. You may have children. The first step is to realize that you are a battered woman and it is not going to get better. The longer you live in self-denial, the worse it may get for you as well as for your children. If you can, talk to a professional counselor, a minister, a priest, or a rabbi about your situation.

Second, seek a safe haven either in the home of someone you trust or a shelter for battered women. You may be better protected from your abusive partner by living in a shelter whose staff is experienced with dealing with violent families. Unfortunately, there are not many shelters available. In Los Angeles County, for example, where police received more than 67,000 domestic calls in 1993, there are approximately 290 shelter beds.

Most shelters will be able to provide you with immediate psychological counseling, as well as legal counseling, on how to file a petition for a restraining order against your abusive partner, if you are in immediate danger.

Some states charge for filing a restraining order while others do not, or allow deferred payment. Even with cases in which an advance payment is required, the judge can order the offending partner to reimburse the victim.

A judge will immediately review your petition for a restraining order and decide if you are in "clear and present danger" of domestic violence. You don't need any witness or evidence of injury. Usually your sworn statement is sufficient. If you've made any previous calls to the police, the judge will also review those reports.

If you're in immediate danger, the judge may issue the restraining order *ex parte,* which means without giving notice to the other party. Because you may be in danger, usually your location is kept confidential by the court or at least until your partner is served with the injunction. The *ex parte* injunction is good until the time needed to schedule a formal hearing. After the hearing, the judge can extend the restraining order for six months to one year. The injunction typically prohibits your partner from coming to the shelter, your home, or place of employment. If he habitually drives by these locations, the judge may forbid him from coming within a designated distance of these places.

But, a restraining order may not necessarily protect you against future violence. According to Circuit Court Judge Raymond T. McNeal for Marion County, Florida, protection "depends on how well they (restraining orders) are enforced by courts and by law enforcement. Enforcement options vary from state to state and from jurisdiction to jurisdiction. Violation of a restraining order may be punished by civil contempt in thirty-one states, and by criminal contempt in twenty-one states. Violation of a restraining order is a misdemeanor in thirty-five states. These enforcement options mean little unless victims have a simplified procedure for prosecuting the abuser for contempt of court. Enforcement by contempt is important because laws limit law enforcement's authority to make an arrest. For example, if an abuser violates a restraining order by coming to the victim's home, but leaves before officers arrive, they will not be able to arrest him. Most states require the officer to witness the offense if it is not a felony. However, if the abuser breaks into the victim's home, assaults her, and leaves before the officers arrive, they can arrest him. Breaking and entering is a felony. If the abuser is not arrested, the victim can request the prosecuting attorney to issue a warrant for the abuser's arrest. Additionally, the victim can file a motion for civil or criminal contempt of court."

Restraining orders work best when the judge advises both the abuser and the victim at the hearing that domestic violence is a crime and that the order will be enforced by the court, with or without the consent of the victim.

Signs to Watch for if You Plan to Marry

Are there signs to look for if the man you are going to marry is a potential wife-beater? Yes, there are, and most women ignore them. Find out his family's history. Studies strongly indicate that men who physically abuse their wives or partners were raised in violent households. Either they were abused or their mothers were abused. Abuse is a learned behavior. If he experienced family violence, you need to discuss it with him and then seek professional couples-counseling. Or, no matter how difficult it may be, you may want to discontinue the relationship. Remember, physical abuse does not always happen immediately in a marriage. It can take months before he strikes.

Another indicator is alcohol abuse. Oftentimes, an alcohol abuser is also a wife abuser. Encourage him to go to Alcoholics Anonymous and you may want to go to Al-Anon. Also, consider abandoning the relationship.

If you decide to break up, be aware that he *could* stalk you. (See information on stalking. Stalking laws are different from domestic-violence laws, although they usually work in tandem.)

If You're Not Physically Abused, You Can Help

If you're not a victim of spouse abuse, support your local shelters by donating money, food, and clothing (shelters are non-profit organizations and donations are tax-deductible), and possibly your time. Also, lobby your state legislators for stronger spouse-abuse laws and more funding of shelters.

Violence in the Workplace

There is a disturbing new trend in America: office violence. Every couple of months, we read in the newspaper or see a report on CNN about a disgruntled worker who walked into his workplace and killed his boss and some of his co-workers. A recent study showed that one in thirty Americans will be hurt in an attack at work. Murder was the top cause of workplace death for women and the third leading cause for all workers, according to the National Institute for Occupational Safety and Health. The National Association of Psychiatric Health Systems estimated that each year as many as 2 to 3 percent of adults (5 million people) suffer mental disorders that keep them from normally associating with co-workers and strangers.

If a co-worker fits the following profile, write a carefully worded statement to the head of your personnel department, specifying examples of the co-worker's violent or potentially violent behavior. Don't discuss the matter with other co-workers. If the personnel department ignores your complaint, talk to your supervisor. If you still don't get a satisfactory response, you may want to think about looking for a new job. Even the police can't help you until the person breaks the law.

Profile of a Potentially Violent Person

- Usually, but not always, a white male in his thirties or forties.
- Attracted to weaponry and talks about weapons.
- Does not take authority well and is a loner with no close family or friends.
- Usually a heavy drinker or drug user.
- Has numerous problems, including divorce, family deaths, financial setbacks, and job difficulties.
- Discusses violent dreams and desires, then makes threats.

Office Romeos

When you first begin a new job, a female colleague may warn you of certain co-workers' sexual office conduct. Heed her warning. She probably knows of or may have had a bad experience. Avoid any close contact with these usually charming office romeos, who seem to like to help newcomers.

Beware of a co-worker who pursues you relentlessly. Start by telling him you have a boyfriend who is big, a weight lifter, and a police officer. Hopefully, that will do the trick, but it may not. If he's obsessed with you, he may call you at home (see Chapter 3 on stopping obscene or annoyance phone calls) or even stalk you. If he continues to pursue you, contact the police and file a restraining order, and be prepared to take defensive measures, which may include carrying a gun. If you feel in imminent danger and can think of no way to get away from him, you may have to take the drastic step of quitting your job and moving out of the city. That sounds crazy, but I've met a number of women in my seminars who have been stalked for months and left with no other choice than to leave their homes and start a new life.

If You Are Being Stalked

Experts project that 5 percent of people in the United States will be stalked at some time in their lives and that as many as 200,000 Americans display stalking traits. Seventy-five to eighty percent of stalking involves people who were former lovers or husbands.

Thirty-six states have legislated antistalking laws. Other states have similar laws under consideration. Also, a federal antistalking law has been proposed that would not preempt state legislation and would be applicable only when states lines have been crossed or mail or telephone services have been used in the stalking process.

If you are being stalked, don't think that your stalker will stop. Take immediate precautions.

Refrain from communicating with the stalker. Don't attempt to reason with the stalker. Change your phone number and request that it be unlisted. Also, purchase a telephone answering machine to screen calls.

Report all suspected stalking to police and tell them to document the incident even if they feel it is too minor for an arrest. Also, keep your own diary with dates and times of each occurrence and record any witnesses.

Tell friends, relatives, and business associates that you are being stalked. In case of an emergency, develop a code word with these people to let them know that you are in imminent danger.

If possible, videotape or tape-record the stalking. Most stalking laws require more than one episode, and if you go to court, documentation will help establish that you were stalked.

Obtain a restraining order. If the terms of the order are breached, contact the police and sign an arrest warrant.

If you feel your life is endangered, hire a bodyguard, move, change jobs, or leave the area. If you decide to arm yourself, do take a safety and self-defense gun course.

High-Risk Professions

There are certain professions that expose women to more danger than others. These jobs may require a woman to work alone, at night, or in an unsafe area. Real estate agents, hospital workers, and traveling saleswomen head the high-risk list, so I'm going to focus on these three professions. However, many of the tips will pertain to others of you as well.

Real Estate Agents

It's kept quiet in the real estate industry, but there are countless stories of agents who are robbed, raped, or murdered while they are showing properties to strangers and meeting potential sellers.

If you are a real estate agent, I recommend that you own a portable cellular phone and develop a buddy system with another agent in your office. Work as a team. Keep each other informed of your whereabouts throughout the day.

I suggest you consider carrying some sort of protection—pepper spray, a mini-baton, or even a handgun. If you don't want to go to the extreme of buying a gun, think about getting a dog, preferably a big one that is well trained. Take it with you wherever you go, even when you sit at an open house. If the seller objects to the dog's presence, explain to him or her that the dog may help deter a criminal from taking any of their personal property. You should also make the seller aware that criminals often go to open houses to case a home and check out its alarm system.

One Los Angeles real estate agent says that some men think looking at properties with a real estate agent is a good way to meet women. "They think they are out on a date," she says. "And it's true, there are some agents who end up going out with their clients. So that helps perpetuate the impression that real estate agents are easy marks."

Often, men come into this agent's office and look around first, checking out the agents before they pick one. "We have a couple of very pretty women who work in our office," she says.

"And we get guys coming in who have seen one of them coming out of the office or out showing a house and they'll ask for the 'pretty blonde who works here.' It's tough. It's like any service-oriented industry. You leave yourself open to trouble, but even more so because you don't always get to do your work in a public place."

In my seminars, I've talked to many real estate agents who have had bad experiences, and with their help, I've come up with some tips that can help you avoid trouble. They may sound overly cautious—and maybe they are—but they are good to keep in mind.

- •When a potential buyer telephones you, get the person's name, business and home phone numbers, and addresses. Even though you're eager to make a sale, don't set up an appointment immediately. Tell the potential client you'll call back shortly. Then, call the person's business number. If the person says something that makes you suspicious, you may want to try to speak with a supervisor or someone in the personnel department to verify what the person does at the office.
- •Your first appointment with a prospective client should be in your office, where you can introduce him to your co-workers. While a legitimate buyer will be relaxed meeting with other brokers, a fraudulent one may feel paranoid knowing that he can later be identified.
- •When you go to the site of the property, don't go in the same car. Have her follow you in her car and take note of the make of her car and its license plate number.
- •If the potential buyer is staying in a hotel and claims to be an out-of-towner, your chances of checking him out diminish. But you can still try. Ask personal questions. Find out where he lives and get home and business numbers. Inquire whether his wife will be accompanying

him when you show him properties. If you don't get satisfactory answers, you may want to pass on him. But whatever you do, don't pick him up at the hotel. If he says he doesn't have a car, tell him to take a taxi to your office.

- •Once you're inside a property you're showing, unlock all the dead-bolt locks so that you can exit quickly if you have to. Know your possible escape routes. Finally, always walk behind your client. This allows you to watch him or her at all times.
- •Don't be fooled by anyone's appearance. Many criminals, including hard-core rapists and murderers, appear to be friendly, well-dressed people.
- •Some communities have Realtor Watch programs, which are similar to Neighborhood Watch programs. If none exist in your area, contact the police department for help in forming one.

Doctors, Nurses, and Other Health Care Workers

Hospital parking structures or parking lots are the most hazardous areas for hospital workers as well as hospital visitors. If you work at a hospital or health clinic, be aware of suspicious persons in parking areas. Report them to security and avoid walking in the parking lot alone, which means you should form a buddy system with one or more co-workers so you can arrive and leave the hospital together. The same is true if you take public transportation. Travel in pairs and consider carrying pepper spray and a mini-baton.

When you're inside the hospital, you'll face a different kind of danger. According to Dr. James T. Turner, a clinical psychologist and author of *Handbook of Hospital Security and Safety,* if you are a nurse, especially an emergency room or psychiatric nurse, you need to be particularly careful when treating victims of stabbings, shootings, and fights because a number of these victims are actually carrying weapons themselves. A study done at Martin Luther King, Jr./Drew Medical Center, a public hospital in Los Angeles, revealed that 25 percent of major trauma patients carried knives or guns, which makes it a good idea to have a security person check a trauma patient for concealed weapons before you treat him or her.

In a recent article in *Glamour* magazine, hospital workers talked about some of the security problems they faced. Gay Howard, an R.N. at the University of Chicago, suggested that if your hospital's security was inadequate, nurses should start a "Code white" system so trained employees could be called when a patient "becomes violent and needs to be restrained or sedated." In the same article, a hospital security expert said that hospitals should "install panic buttons or buzzer systems on each floor for nurses." Meanwhile, Dr. Turner encourages hospital administrators to set up an aggression-management course for nurses.

However, don't rely on other people or buttons and buzzers for your safety. If possible, take a self-defense fighting course that includes training in taking weapons away from an attacker.

Those of you who are home health care nurses know that you face a different set of security problems. You have to deal with strangers in *their* environment, not yours. Sometimes this environment isn't the best, and neither is the patient or the people that live with him. Therefore, I suggest that before you go to see a new patient, call the house and talk to the patient or a member of the patient's family. Try to assess the situation and the neighborhood. If you feel uncomfortable about anything, call your supervisor and discuss your feelings. You may not want to take the job. But if you do take it, and you know you'll be going to an unsafe neighborhood, you should certainly carry a mini-baton and pepper spray.

One home care nurse told me that a number of home care

nurses now carry cellular phones. "It's good to have a cellular phone handy in case of an emergency," she said. "But I also use it to inform a patient that I have arrived at his or her house or apartment complex. Sometimes, if I'm in an area that I'm unsure about, I'll have the patient or someone who is staying with the patient come out to my car and escort me into the building."

Traveling Saleswomen

If you spend your days traveling on the road and your nights sleeping in hotels and motels, you are at risk. For about six months, I was a pharmaceutical representative for my father's surgical supply company, so I understand a little bit about what this kind of lifestyle is like. In general, I had a fairly fixed schedule and made visits to the same places on a monthly or bimonthly basis. What I learned is that your most important safety net is to always go to the same hotels, motels, restaurants, and gas stations, so that the proprietors get to know you. That way, if an emergency situation arises, they will be more likely to react quickly and help you.

There are two other rules that I tried to follow when I was on the road for my father's company. I tried to arrive at my destinations before dark, and I made sure my car was in good working condition. I had it tuned up regularly so I wouldn't end up getting stranded along the side of some road in the middle of nowhere. I also checked my spare tire from time to time to make sure the pressure was good.

At the suggestion of an experienced traveling saleswoman, I put together an emergency kit that I kept in the trunk of my car. This included flares, a large flashlight, a blanket, bottled water, freeze-dried food, matches, and medical supplies. She also suggested I install a CB radio, and although I didn't, I now think that either a CB radio or a cellular phone is a must for any traveling saleswoman. I would also carry pepper spray and even

consider carrying a handgun. But before I bought a gun, I'd
check the gun laws in my state or the states where I was going
to travel the most.

As I said earlier, public rest rooms at highway stops are dangerous. You're going to laugh when I tell you this, but self-defense experts Craig Fox Huber and Don Paul recommend
keeping an empty tennis ball can with a sealable lid stored under your seat. They say if you have to go to the bathroom badly
and can't find somewhere safe to stop, you can relieve yourself
into the can. It's also good to have in case you get stuck in a traffic jam.

CHAPTER SIX

Security While Traveling

OVER THE LAST twenty years, women's travel, especially business travel, has been on the rise, and today nearly 40 percent of all business travelers are women. That's terrific, but as we know, there is a certain uneasiness we all feel when traveling. On a trip, we often find ourselves entering a completely new environment, which makes us feel even more vulnerable to the potential dangers we worried about at home in our semi-controlled environments. We've heard the stories of theft and terrorism abroad, and here, in the United States, we've heard of women travelers who have been raped in their hotel rooms and even murdered. Those are real fears. But the point is, we don't have to feel as vulnerable as we might when we travel, because we can learn to control the new environments we encounter. How? By using some of the same protection strategies we use during our daily lives at home.

Hotel Security

When I walk into a large hotel, I often feel like I've dropped into a mini-city filled with hundreds of people from all over the world. Most of these people are law-abiding citizens, but just like in any city, there are always going to be a few that aren't. The only problem is that hotels, which are built for openness and hospitality, are essentially ill equipped to deal with criminals, especially when many hotel operators and managers— even at the best hotels—play the odds and scrimp on security. That's why you have to take your own precautions, starting from the moment you arrive at a hotel. If you are arriving by car and you arrive after dark, park as close as you can to the main entrance or registration area, which will minimize the chances of your car being broken into during the time you spend checking in.

Many hotels offer valet parking or may have a staff member available to relocate your car during check-in. That's fine, but make sure you are giving your keys to a valet parker or a representative of the hotel, because occasionally, car thieves will pose as hotel employees. You might want to check for the hotel's emblem on the attendant's jacket or ask him a few questions concerning where your car will be taken. There's no way to be absolutely sure he is who he says he is, but if you feel uneasy for any reason, keep your keys and talk to someone inside the hotel who can verify that the attendant is associated with the hotel.

If, after you check in, you have to drive to a spot some distance away in a large parking lot or garage, check to see if that area appears well lighted and safe. If it isn't, you might want to drive back to the front of the hotel and ask someone from the hotel's security staff to accompany you.

Also, beware that parking in a parking space marked with your room number has one drawback. If someone has seen you come in and park, he will now know your room number. And that's why it's important to try to remain anonymous when you check in. If you can, use a different last name or register with your first initial and last name only, leaving the Mr./Mrs. designation blank.

When you receive a key, the front desk clerk may say "Ms. Anderson, here's your room key. You're staying in room 1107, the elevators are behind you." Or the clerk may inform the bell-man, "Ms. Anderson is staying in room 1107, please help her with her luggage." That's not good. The clerk has not only given anybody within earshot your name and the room you're staying in, but he's informed them you are traveling alone. Today, more and more hotels are taking precautions against making announcements like this, because, in the past, women found themselves getting calls from strange men who'd simply been standing near them when they were checking in. But if you feel that your privacy has been compromised in any way, don't be afraid to discreetly inform the clerk that he shouldn't have stated your name and room number so loudly and that you wish to be assigned to a different room. Taking this action may seem a little paranoid, but it's better than being afraid that someone you don't know will knock on your door in the middle of the night.

To a certain degree, everything comes down to your own best judgment. I don't expect you to follow my instructions to a T, but it's important for you to be aware of as many things that could leave you open to possible danger. For instance, it may seem silly when you first enter your room to ask a bellman or hotel staffer to stay there until you're sure that it's *empty*, but remember, there have been incidents where a rapist or Peeping Tom has gotten into a room and hidden there for several hours, waiting for a victim to arrive. So you might want to check the closets, bathroom, and underneath the beds. Also check any locks in the room, whether they be door, window, or in-room safe locks. Make sure they work, and if they don't, report the problem to the front desk and asked to be moved to another room.

Door Keys

Use extra caution when staying in hotels that do not have a re-programmable door lock system for their rooms. Reprogrammable locks allow for frequent and rapid rekeying of guest rooms, which make previous guests' keys useless. These types of locks are generally easy to identify, because the key that you get for them is about the same size and shape of a credit card and is made of paper, plastic, or metal. It may or may not have holes punched in it.

Most luxury hotels have reprogrammable keys. Others, like Holiday Inn Worldwide, which recently announced plans to outfit each of its more than 1,500 hotels in North America with electronic door locks, are gradually following suit. While approximately one-third of Holiday Inn's hotels already have electronic locking systems, this plan will cover all the hotels by January 1, 1996. Holiday Inn cards will bear no room number, be rekeyed with each new guest, and provide a computerized record of who entered the rooms and when.

Safe Deposit Boxes

In general, it's a good idea to check your valuables into the hotel's safe or one of their safe deposit boxes. When you do, put them in a sealed envelope and be sure to get a receipt with the amount written on it. Some travelers are nervous about putting their jewelry and money into these safes, but Michele Kelley, a spokesperson for the American Hotel and Motel Association, assures us that safe deposit vaults are trustworthy and recommends their usage. However, other industry insiders admit that armed robberies have occurred in some of America's four-star hotels and suggest that you think twice about storing expensive jewelry in hotel safes, especially if you don't have your own personal insurance on these valuables.

The problem is each state and every country has its own law that limits the hotel's liability to anywhere from $250 to $2,000. To further complicate matters, hotels are not bound to reimburse you for the maximum amount of liability. In New York State, for instance, a hotel's liability is limited to $1,500, but the Holiday Inn next to JFK Airport will insure you only up to $500. However, if you specify in writing the full value of your property when you request a safe deposit box, the hotel may increase the liability. So check all the numbers before you hand over your valuables.

You may want to store your jewelry in one of the hotel's in-room safes. If you plan on doing so, you should check to see where your room is located. If it's isolated from the rest of the rooms or has sliding glass doors at ground level, you may want to request a room change. Most hotel security experts believe that the rooms closest to the elevators are the safest, and those rooms closest to back stairs and entrances are the riskiest. However, the rooms near elevators can be noisy.

Fire Precaution

If a fire breaks out, you're better off being on a lower floor, because most fire rescue equipment doesn't reach higher than the sixth floor. But you don't want to be too low, because a burglar is more likely to rob a room on the first two floors. So I advise requesting a room between the third and sixth floors.

Other than that, there isn't much you can do to prepare yourself for a fire except to familiarize yourself with your door locks and the fire exits on your floor. You should take a quick look to see if the nearest exits are clear and ready for use, because you don't want to discover they're blocked or stuck at four o'clock in the morning with smoke in the air and the fire alarm sounding. I also think it's important to keep your room key where you can easily find it, even in the dark. If there is a fire, don't leave your room without your key, because you may have to return to your room if the exits are unusable.

Keep Strangers Out!

Before you open your door to any strangers, keep this thought in mind: In almost 100 percent of the assault, robbery, and rape incidents at hotels, the victim voluntarily opened the door to the attacker. Often, this happened because the attacker was impersonating a member of the hotel staff, usually a room service worker, maintenance person, or hotel security person. For example, some criminals will pick up the breakfast request menu you left hanging outside your door, then come back later, knock on your door, and say your breakfast is ready. Some have phony breakfasts for you, others don't, but the result is the same. As soon as you open the door, he will rush in and overcome you.

That's why I urge women not to open their doors to any stranger. If you are going to request anything, call the front desk and ask for it. If you really want to be careful, you might have the clerk tell you the name of the person he or she is going to send up. That way, when the person knocks on the door, you can verify the name.

But what about the maid? Most of you, I suspect, would open the door for a maid, especially if she was a woman. It's a judgment call, as I said before, but if you want to be extra cautious (maybe because you have something valuable in the room), I suggest you call the front desk in the morning and ask for your room be made up at a particular time that's convenient for you. Then stay in the room while it's being cleaned.

Finally, never leave your door open, even if you're just going down the hall to the ice or vending machines. Also, be aware that the signs you hang on the outside of you door send a message to criminals:

- •A Please Make Up This Room sign on the outside of your door indicates you aren't around and could invite thieves.
- •Conversely, a Do Not Disturb sign on the outside of your door indicates you are around, which should deter them.

Hallways and Elevators

While most hotel hallways and elevators are safe, particularly during the day and early evening hours, always be aware of your surroundings. If there is a person who makes you feel uncomfortable, get away from him or her. Take the elevator, go to the lobby, even ask the bellman to accompany you to your room. If you're accosted in a hallway, yell "Fire! Everybody out of the rooms," rather than "Help," because the fire warning gets more attention.

Lights On!

When you leave your hotel room, leave a light on as well as the TV. If the light is off when you come back, proceed cautiously, because it can only mean one of two things: Either the maid turned the light off or there is someone in the room waiting for you. In all likelihood, it is the first scenario, though in most hotels, personnel are trained not turn off single lights when they are left on by hotel guests. So if you feel threatened—again, this is a judgment call—you should not hesitate to contact the hotel's security and have them check the room for you.

Once you're in your room, if you want to feel more secure, you can wedge something under the door to prevent it from being opened; a rubber stop works well, but what's even better is a portable Door Jammer (see Chapter 3). There are also portable burglar alarms, but I don't advise them because many of them are prone to false alarms from vibrations.

Health Clubs

Before using a hotel's health club or gym, check it out. If it's in a remote area of the hotel or poorly attended, it can become a potentially dangerous spot. Also, beware of peepholes behind mirrors; low-rise motels with a maintenance corridor behind rooms are especially be susceptible. Recently, there have been a number of legal cases involving voyeurism.

Conference Rooms

If you're attending a meeting in a hotel, don't leave your purse or briefcase unattended in a conference room, especially during a recess or lunch break. Because most conference rooms are near public areas, like the lobby, virtually anyone can enter the room, making conference room thefts quite common.

Conventions

If you're at a convention, be aware that criminals think conventioneers have lots of money and are easy marks, and they're probably right. So when you leave the convention site or hotel, remove your convention badge. Not only does it label you as a stranger to the city, but it tells people your name, company, and often the hotel you're staying at. Conventions are great environments for scams and cons, so the best advice is: Beware of strangers, and don't let your guard down.

Out on the Town

If you decide to go out alone at night and plan to walk or use public transportation, talk with a woman at the hotel's front desk to determine if it's safe to walk alone on the city's streets. Wear flat shoes or sneakers, and carry your heels in a bag. It's much easier to run in flat shoes. When walking alone, walk against the traffic, and if you feel uncomfortable, walk in the street (on the shoulder) rather than on the sidewalk. It's actually safer to walk in a street if someone is lurking in an alleyway or building entry way. Before you take a cab somewhere, make sure you find out whether there will be a cab to take you back from the restaurant at a later hour. You don't want to get stranded anywhere.

Money Belts

I'm a great believer in carrying money, credit cards, passports, and other valuables in money belts, which fit comfortably around your waist underneath a blouse or sweater. That way you can keep a small amount of money, makeup, and other incidentals in your purse or waist pack without worrying that your trip will become jeopardized if your purse is snatched. But beware, criminals are not stupid and know that tourists wear money belts, so it's a good idea to carry a purse and use it is a decoy. Money belts are inexpensive and can be purchased wherever luggage is sold.

Documents

Leave a photocopy of important documents like the photo page of your passport, travelers checks, credit card numbers, and any prescriptions at home and in your office. Carry another set of copies with you, but not in your purse, in case it's stolen. You should also carry a card that has all your vital information on it, including the name and phone number of whom to contact in case of an emergency, medical allergies you have, and any prescription medicine you are taking. If you use a travel agency, carry a card with its 800 emergency line. It may come in handy, especially if you're traveling abroad.

World Crime Report

The Dutch Ministry of Justice's Criminal Victimization in the Industrialized World Survey of 55,000 in twenty industrialized countries found the following:

- The countries where people are the most worried about crime are, in order, New Zealand, Australia, England, the Czech Republic, and the United States.
- Women were at higher risk from sexual assault in Australia and Canada than in the United States.
- Between 3 and 6 percent of the women surveyed in Germany and Poland reported that they had been sexually assaulted.

Fake Passports and Documents for Threatened Corporate Executives

Although the U.S. government is making it harder to counterfeit passports, Virginia-based Security Dynamics International provides fake passports and documents for government and corporate executives traveling abroad. In a life-threatening or kidnapping situation, a foreign-traveling executive can conceal his or her real passport and present a surrogate passport, which may save his or her life in the event the kidnappers are from a political faction that is anti-American.

Security Dynamics International can put together a package of documents tailored to a particular individual. According to *Security* magazine, the company creates "passports and other supporting documents showing an originating but nonexistent country—typically a country that might have recently changed its name—complete with entry and exit stamps, as well as visas so as to give an authentic appearance. The firm updates the fakes with recent visas and entry/exit stamps on a regular basis." A library card, work ID, and other supporting documents are also helpful in providing a convincing cover.

Possessing the phony passport and documents isn't a crime, according to *Security* magazine. "But using them fraudulently is," says Security Dynamics International's president. "So our clients know to use the surrogate documents only in extreme situations."

Transportation

Cars

If you are visiting a big city, I don't recommend renting a car unless you know the city well. Take a taxi or rent a limousine, which may sound exorbitant, but in many instances, limousine or private car services are actually less expensive than taxis. If you are going to take a taxi, ask the hotel concierge or front desk clerk what the best route to your destination is. If you engage in small talk with the driver, be savvy and make believe that you know the city or actually live in the city. As many of you well know, unscrupulous cab drivers are capable of taking out-of-towners several miles out of their way to increase their fares. Also, it's a good idea to lock the back doors and put your purse or briefcase on the floor of the taxi so that they can't be seen by pedestrians. Regrettably, in some countries, many taxis' doors don't lock and the windows can't be closed because there is no air-conditioning, so stay alert.

If you rent a car, ask for one that has no window or bumper stickers, license plates, or license plate holders that identify it as a rental car. After an increased number of crimes against tourists, many companies are starting to remove them, but a lot of rental cars still have markings that identify them as such. If this is a concern for you, I suggest calling ahead of time and finding a company that has unmarked cars.

Once you leave the rental company parking lot, watch for anyone who may be following you. If you're concerned that someone is, drive to a public place immediately. In Chapter 4, I talked about what to do in case you are being followed on the highway, but I will repeat myself. In such a situation, keep driving and do not pull over. Many rental companies, especially in big tourist spots like Florida, have started giving out instructions on what areas to avoid and how to act if you are being followed, so read them carefully. Some instruction sheets will tell you not to leave any maps on the seat, as this indicates you are a tourist, and to keep all of your belongings locked in the trunk. However, if you have anything valuable, take it with you when you leave the car.

Buses and Trains

Traveling by bus or train in the United States and in many parts of the world has its risks, especially in terms of theft. Probably the most hazardous point is the terminal itself, because a thief knows you probably won't discover a robbery until you've boarded your bus or train, which makes it difficult, if not impossible, for you to notify the police.

That's why, when you're standing in line to purchase a ticket, it's important to keep your distance from strangers and not to get into conversations. If you have to wait for a bus or train in the terminal, sit against a wall and watch your belongings. It's not a good idea to take a nap unless you have a friend watching your luggage or you have a portable motion alarm, such as the Quorum Alert, attached to your suitcase, so if it's touched, you will be woken up.

Once you're on the bus or train, if you don't feel comfortable where you're seated or who you're seated next to, get up and move. On a bus, it's probably safer to sit as close as possible to the driver, but in developing countries, you have to be concerned about hijackers and robbers getting on the bus.

Airplanes

There is some truth to United Airline's slogan, "fly the friendly skies," because airline travel is undoubtedly the safest way for you to get from one place to the next. However, your luggage might not agree. Too often it doesn't make it in the condition it left in, and every once in a while, it disappears altogether. So, rule number 1 is travel light, and if you can, limit your luggage to the two small carry-ons you are allowed to bring on the plane. One of the best and easiest kinds of luggage to carry is roller-board luggage, which was originally designed by a pilot and first used by flight attendants. These rectangular soft-sided suitcases, complete with wheels and a retractable handle, fit in most overhead storage compartments. Two of the best manufacturers are Boyt and Travelpro.

Another rule is use inexpensive luggage when traveling. Although you may like the looks of Louis Vuitton and Hartmann bags, they stand out on a conveyor belt and will attract thieves, who, I assure you, are as brand-conscious as you are. If your suitcases have locks, use them, but the problem is they are usually so poorly made that a baggage handler can easily break them off the bag with a screwdriver. Also, people who steal luggage often clip outside ID tags off, so it's a good idea to only write your name and a business number on an outside tag, then provide more substantial information on a tag that you place inside the bag and can later use to identify the bag in case it is lost and needs to be claimed.

Self defense experts Craig Fox Huber and former Green Beret Don Paul suggest labeling the outside of suitcases with stickers that say such things as Los Angeles Police Department Property or Contagious Medical Supplies to scare off potential thieves. They also recommend dropping a little hot candle wax on your suitcase locks to make a seal. That way, when you get your bag back, you'll be able to determine if it was opened since you checked it. Another little trick they suggest is to place a match inside your case with one end protruding just outside the case when it's closed. If the match is gone when you retrieve the bag, you know it's been opened.

Be cautious of purse snatchers while you're in the airport. You're most at risk to having items stolen while you're sitting in the terminal waiting for your plane, so if you can afford it, it's a good idea to be a member of one of the airline's private clubs. Although they are generally pretty safe, don't be lulled into a sense of security, because there have been thefts reported even from there. Once you're on the plane, you're fairly secure. If you go to sleep, keep your handbag on your lap, and when you move around the cabin or go to the toilet, always take your purse with you. Also, it's a good idea to check whether you have all your belongings just before the plane goes into its final descent. That way, if something's missing, you can notify a flight attendant and ask her to make an announcement while the thief is still on board. You'd be surprised what mysteriously turns up after an announcement has been made that something has been stolen.

Travel Advisory

Two governmental agencies—the State and Transportation Departments—offer security services for U.S. citizens traveling abroad.

The State Department's Bureau of Consular Affairs has updated foreign travel information and advisories. They are available by telephone, fax-back (if you have a fax machine), and computer modem.

The Transportation Department has a toll-free travel advisory service that warns of "known, credible, current threats" to airlines and public transportation systems in the United States and abroad.

Government Travel Advice

From the State Department's Bureau of Consular Affairs:
By phone: (202) 647-5225
By fax-back: (202) 647-3000
By modem: (202) 647-9225

From the Transportation Department's Travel
Advisory Service:
By phone: (800) 221-0673
SOURCE: *Security* magazine.

Airport Parking Lots

Airport parking lots are as unsafe as any other parking lots. If you can, have a friend drive you to the airport, take a taxi, or use one of the many reputable airport minivans. Probably the most dangerous lots are the long-term parking lots, because many of them are huge and have few people walking around them. If you need to leave your car in a long-term lot, I suggest you park right next to a shuttle stop, so if you feel threatened in any way, you can ask the shuttle's driver to wait a moment until you get in your car and drive away. If you only need to leave your car for a day or two, you might want to use one of the many airport hotels' parking lots. In general, they have valet parking and offer regularly scheduled van service to and from the airlines' terminals.

Backpacking and Camping

Camping and backpacking are becoming increasingly popular activities for women. You'd think that women would feel less afraid of so-called urban crime when taking a trip to the great outdoors, but according to several female rangers from the National Park Service, rape and harassment are common concerns of women preparing to take camping trips. In 1992, the National Parks Service Annual Law Enforcement Program reported that there were 56 reported rapes, 14 attempted rapes, and 836 burglaries in the 350 National Park Service areas around the country that are visited by almost 80 million people annually. That's not a crime epidemic, but if you're in the wrong place at the wrong time, you could become a statistic.

According to Mona Davis, a park ranger at Yellowstone National Park since 1977, most of the rapes took place in motels and lodges on park service property. She says that the problems usually occur when there is a mix of crowds and alcohol.

In general, it's not a good idea to backpack or camp alone, but if you want to go alone and the park allows dogs, take one for protection. Whether you travel alone or in a group, I suggest that you check in with the ranger station and leave your itinerary with them before you set off into the wilderness. You should also tell a friend at home where you are going and give him or her the ranger station phone number (get it from the National Park Service) in case you don't return when you're supposed to.

As for clothes, I suggest dressing like a man. Hide your hair under a man's hat and wear a man's jacket and shirt. That way, at a distance at least, you'll look like a man and be safer.

Carry pepper spray on a belt clip. It's highly effective against humans as well as animals. Also, carry "mugger money." Have two wallets with you, and if you're held up, give the mugger the wallet that only has $20 in it. Your "real money," credit cards, and other valuables should be kept in a money belt underneath your shirt.

You are more vulnerable to attack at night, when you're restricted from movement by your sleeping bag. So, for greater freedom, you may want to buy a German surplus army sleeping bag, which has arms and a zipper at the bottom so you can poke your feet out and walk around if you have to. Although it isn't down-filled, it is warm and waterproof.

If you're sleeping in a camper or recreation vehicle, you can purchase a small battery-powered motion detector made by Detec Security Systems. When an intruder or bear enters your campsite, the detector transmits a signal to a receiver inside your vehicle, which sets off an alarm. The device also provides curtain coverage to eliminate detection of small animals.

If you're camping in bear country, you're probably more at risk from bear attack than human attack. The California Department of Fish and Game recommends the following safety tips:

- Don't leave food or anything smelly outside. Place garbage in bear-proof cans. Keep your campsite clean, and cook at least 100 yards downwind from your tent.
- Store your food and toiletries in a vehicle trunk or suspend them from a tree at least ten feet from the ground and four feet from the tree's trunk.
- Never sleep in the clothes you wore while cooking.

CHAPTER SEVEN

Fighting Back

MORE THAN TEN years ago, the general consensus among police officers was that if a woman was attacked, she was best off not resisting. In the last few years, however, attitudes have changed, and now most police and self-defense experts recommend that women fight back both verbally and physically. Recent studies show that even an untrained woman who demonstrates real anger during an attack is less likely to be harmed than a woman who remains passive.

Two studies, one funded by Brandeis University, the other by the National Institute of Mental Health, conclusively showed that the women most apt to be raped were those who did not fight back. In the second study, Dr. Pauline Bart, a sociologist at the University of Illinois, interviewed ninety-four women who had been attacked. Of the ninety-four, forty-three had been raped and fifty-one had avoided being raped. The study found that, on the average, the women who had avoided rape had used more and different strategies of resistance—fleeing, yelling, and fighting—than those who had been raped. The study also showed that the resisting women did not significantly increase their likelihood of serious injury by fighting back. Furthermore, Dr. Bart found that verbal techniques such as reasoning had proved useless and that most of the women who had pleaded not to be harmed had, in fact, been raped.

The trouble is, it isn't so easy to fight back. Often, when a woman is about to be assaulted, she becomes so fearful that she denies what's about to happen to her. She literally removes herself from the scene and ends up watching the confrontation as if she weren't there. Similarly, some women become paralyzed when they're attacked. Part of the problem, says Dr. Carl H. Shubs, a psychologist and trauma specialist in private practice in Los Angeles, is that many women aren't programmed to be aggressive.

He explains: "If you grew up with the message, 'it's not nice to be aggressive,' then you are programmed not to allow your emotions to move outward, toward someone else, which is what *aggressive* really means. You are not likely to be able to reach out for what you want or strike out to defend yourself. All the energy and emotion stays directed inward instead."

Fear can be stifling, and you must come to terms with it in order to learn effectively and execute self defense skills. However, you don't want to be fearless, because you don't want to put yourself in a dangerous situation, like walking at night in an alley or in a park. It's okay to have fear; it doesn't make you a weak person, and it can actually tell you that danger is present. It can also give you incredible strength if you learn to turn it into anger when you have to. That's the key to defending yourself, because you'd be surprised how strong you can be when you're angry.

There is fright in all sorts of situations. This is the mind frightened by the unexpected.

If you can seize the moment of fright, you can take advantage of it to win.

—Miyamoto Musashi, "Five Scroll," *Book of Five Spheres* (from *The Japanese Art of War* by Thomas Cleary)

Verbal Self-Defense

If you ever met Nancy Salinger, you'd never think she could yell profanities in a supermarket parking lot in pristine Newport Beach, California. A petite, refined woman in her early fifties, Nancy was pushing a shopping cart full of groceries toward her car when two young men approached her and asked if they could help her. Sensing that the pair wasn't really interested in helping, she said forcefully, "Get the fuck out of here." They froze right in their tracks, a look of surprise coming over their faces. Then, after she had passed them, she heard one say, "Bitch," but they didn't follow her. When she got to her Mercedes, she looked back and saw them leaving the area.

"I never thought I could swear like I did," she says. "I felt in control. I really wasn't scared."

Yelling at someone who is harassing you or about to attack you can often be effective in preventing the harassment from escalating because it draws attention to the situation, especially when there are other people around who can possibly help you. Also, when you're aggressive and maintain an authoritative attitude and posture, you may be able to spook a would-be attacker—he is scared, too, and may not want to deal with a combative woman.

Our natural reaction is to yell for help, but the problem is most bystanders don't respond to such pleas. There have been numerous cases reported of a crowd watching a person get assaulted or robbed and done nothing to help him or her. That's why it's better to yell such commands as "Back off," "Get away," "Stop right there," or "I don't know this man, he's harassing me." Not only does this attract attention to your situation, but it puts you on the offensive. However, once you launch this aggressive strategy, you can't retreat, either verbally or physically.

According to Clifford Stewart, a bodyguard and founder of Within Arms Reach (WAR), "Physically backing up puts you into the scared victim role. Backing up takes away your power and gives an attacker more power over you." Backing up, he adds, can also be dangerous. You may find yourself backed into a corner or you may trip and fall. "The only time you should move backward," Stewart says, "is to gain distance for fighting."

Swearing at a potential attacker can also help you establish distance. I learned this tactic years ago when I went to San Quentin Penitentiary to interview rapists for my book *Armed & Female*. One of the convicts, a short man who wore a dark blue knit cap pulled down to his eyebrows, explained to me that women should swear at men who are harassing them. Initially, I was surprised by his suggestion, because I thought such an action would make an attacker even angrier. But he explained that everyone around him swore—his mother, his brothers, his friends—and he and his buddies didn't expect to hear "some nice lady swearing."

Of course, swearing doesn't work all the time. I wouldn't do it if a guy had a knife or a gun pointed at my throat. But it can be effective at other times, especially when you're in a public place and there are other people nearby. I've had a number of reports from my students who have successfully stopped someone from coming any closer to them by swearing. I've done it, too. But I can't tell you exactly when to do it. That's a judgment call, like so much else in personal protection strategies.

As part of my seminar, Women's Empowerment in the '90s, we do an exercise called "Get The Fuck Out Of Here!" We all stand in a large circle, and I act as if I'm a would-be attacker. Looking as mean as possible, I walk up to each woman and stare her in the face. When I do this, the woman I am facing is supposed to stare right back and yell "Get the fuck out of here!"

For some women, this drill is difficult to do at first, and a few of them giggle nervously when I "get in their face." They're not accustomed to swearing in public or swearing at strangers. Many women actually find it easier to get angry and swear at their husbands or boyfriends than to swear at someone who intends to harm them. This exercise helps them get over their reluctance to aggressively face a confrontational situation.

You can practice the swearing drill at home, although it does not have the same impact as doing it with other people around. I recommend that you go into your bathroom and close the door. Then look at yourself in the mirror and practice yelling "Get the fuck out of here!" Look as nasty as possible. Do this exercise for a number of days, then, if you have a friend who's willing to be a guinea pig, do the drill in front of him or her.

Another verbal self-defense drill that I use in my seminar is to teach women how to yell "No!" Yelling "No!" is an extremely useful response when you're attacked because it helps you to keep from freezing up. As I've mentioned earlier, some women become paralyzed when they're assaulted: They hold their breath; they can't scream and can't fight. The best way to break that freeze response is to yell "No!"

In my seminar, after we've done the "Get-The-Fuck-Out-Of-Here!" drill, the women stay in the circle and practice yelling "No!" at me. After they've done both exercises, they're hyped up and can really yell convincingly. Frankly, I wouldn't want to meet some of these women in a parking lot. They sound and look ferocious.

At home, you can practice the "No!" drill just as you practiced the first exercise.

The Option to Fight

Spirit is more important than size! In a real fight few of us will be able to do picture-perfect techniques; however, with the right spirit and attitude, they can be made effective. Your attitude is going to make the difference in determining the outcome of a fight.

In fighting back, keep these principles in mind:

1. You do not deserve to be attacked! Everyone, including women, children, and all sentient beings, has a right to live free of harm. Women must believe they have a right to resist physical assault. Believing this is a fundamental asset. You must believe you are worth defending. It is a *positive action* to stop violence against you or anyone else.
2. There are no rules. A serious, unprovoked assault is not a game or a sport. In fact, aggressors tend to display out-of-control behaviors and have a different set of rules. Human trust is broken when someone attacks another person. You must be prepared to break all usual rules and restraints in your defense. Remember, no one "asks" to be attacked sexually or otherwise.
3. Size doesn't matter! In a life-threatening situation, size and strength are not that important. When survival is at stake, the important qualities to bring to the situation are determination and the capacity to focus your energies.
4. Commitment counts! In fighting back, you need to commit mentally and physically 100 percent to your survival and safety. The combatant who is the most determined has the best chance. That means being

aggressive and following through on your technique. You must be prepared to hurt and disable an assailant. As long as you are not resisting, he is able to continue to attack! Studies have shown that the more things a woman does as early as possible in her defense, the better chance she has of winning. If you are attacking back, he must then be concerned with *his* vulnerability.

Permission to print granted by BAMM Impact, San Carlos, California.

Fighting for Survival

Saundra, a student of mine, reported the following incident. Early one morning Saundra found herself out of cash and decided to go to an ATM machine on a busy street in Los Angeles where she felt relatively safe. After withdrawing $50, she turned around and was confronted by a man who said, "Gimme your money." She froze for a moment and actually thought of handing the $50 to him, but then she saw that he didn't have a weapon, and in flash, she hit him in the nose with the heel of her palm as hard as she could. It was a direct hit. Covering his face with his hands, the man screamed in pain, and Saundra ran. She ran to her car, a block away, and got in and locked all the doors and started the engine. Shaken a bit, but calm, she then drove past the ATM machine, looking for the man so she could get a better description for the police. But he was nowhere to be found. He, too, had run away. "Well," she said to herself, smiling. "I'll be damned. It works!"

Saundra had taken my seminar as well as another self-defense course. After the the incident, she called me up and said,

"I took the classes not really believing that I would ever need to fight because I thought that I was a pretty aware person and wouldn't find myself in trouble. But then it happened, and I have to say I was pretty surprised at how fast I reacted. Before the classes, I never would have been able to have done what I did because I was so fearful of being violated."

Even though you may be like Saundra and take precautions, you, too, may become a target and have to fight back. You may not think that you're capable of fighting back because you don't believe in violence, but remember there is an enormous moral distinction between criminal violence and self-defense. Many women feel that by saying they are nonviolent, they won't become a target of violence. I've heard women actually say, "I've got good karma; nothing will happen to me."

Unfortunately, this spiritual philosophy doesn't always hold up on the streets. I've interviewed hundreds of women who thought they were "good" women, but they were assaulted. Most of them were unprepared to fight. Often, these women take self-protection classes after a violent encounter, determined never to be a victim again. However, tens of thousands of women are enrolling in classes before anything bad happens to them. According to Nancy Brittle of AWARE, "Women are no longer hoping that danger will go away or relying on others for protection. They recognize that the best time to learn to swim is not when the ship is sinking, so they are getting trained *now.*"

As far as I know, the best way to learn fighting skills is to take a self-defense class that makes you fight off an attacker in a mock assault. In these classes, you learn how to strike a mock attacker's face, head, and groin, using full force. Your goal is to knock him out, and you don't have to hold anything back since the mock attacker is wearing sixty pounds of customized protective equipment and a huge, intimidating padded helmet.

Other self defense classes, including traditional martial arts, are good, but if you're not making contact with the attacker and delivering actual blows, you don't know what it's really like to fight. You don't feel your fear, work through it, and come out the victor.

The founder of mock assaults is Matthew Thomas, who began a course called Model Mugging twenty-three years ago after a friend who was a black belt in karate was attacked and raped. Although his friend was well versed in the martial arts, she had never hit anyone with full force or learned to fight on the ground. Upset by her attack, Thomas researched police department records and analyzed 3,000 assaults against women. The first thing he discovered was that men fight women differently from the way they fight with men. When a man attacks a woman, Thomas discovered, he usually knocks her to the ground in six seconds or less. That meant that women not only needed to learn contact fighting, but they needed to learn how to fight from a ground position, using their legs and feet as weapons.

After finishing his research, Thomas started his twenty-hour, four-week course. Since 1970, he has personally trained nearly 5,000 women, been kicked in the head half a million times, had his ribs broken six times, and been knocked out nineteen times. He has also helped develop a number of successful off-shoot programs, including one called Impact Personal Safety. The courses are designed for women of all sizes, ages, and physical fitness levels. Classes run a total of twenty hours and vary in cost according to location (see appendix for further information). They include warm-up exercises, physical technique instruction, and mock attacks that are always followed by a group discussion where students share their experiences. Since 50 percent of the students are survivors of assaults, the mock assaults often trigger memories of prior violent episodes.

In total, 20,000 women have graduated from the courses, and according to Thomas, 300 alumnae have deterred attacks by yelling, while another 80 successfully fought off their assailants, 49 of them "winning" by knockout.

Why is the training so effective? Thomas says, "Muscle memory is the key to success. Basically, the mock assault sets up an adrenaline state under which freeze and flail responses are reconditioned. If that adrenaline state is similarly aroused in a real-life attack, women's bodies respond in ways their muscles remember as being effective: They fight in the no-mind warrior state of reflex action."

A woman thrusting the heel of her palm into the mugger's face.

When I was researching my first book, I took both Model Mugging and IMPACT Personal Safety, and they turned out to be the most empowering experiences of my life. Before that, I never really knew how strong I was or felt the depth of my determination to survive. During the mock assaults, I became so immersed in fighting the mugger that I unconsciously suspended all reality and lived the assault as if it were an actual one. I was ferocious. I swore and kicked the mugger's face and body without thinking. All I wanted to do was knock him out as quickly as possible. (By knock out, I mean knock out in a mock sense. Rarely does a mock attacker, with all his protective gear, actually get knocked out. However, a referee announces when you've delivered a knockout kick or punch and blows her whistle to stop the fight.) After winning a fight, I'd get such a rush, and that feeling of empowerment stays with me all the time.

Lisa Gaeta, executive director of IMPACT Personal Safety, explains what happens during a mock assault. "Once the fight starts, there is no cognitive thought, and somehow, fear is replaced by the will to survive. There is no thinking on the mat, only action and reaction and yelling and fighting—fighting for our lives. You don't really have to work at overcoming fear; it just happens. Keep in mind that the subconscious mind does not know the difference between a real fight and this mock assault. Physiologically your body reacts the same. When you come off the mat, you may not remember what you just did, but your subconscious mind has recorded it. It is recorded as a successful fight in which you saved your life."

Gaeta adds, "Once your body believes it can be attacked and survive, the trauma of the mock assault becomes less acute, the fear becoming less intense each time. As the fear eases up—it never quite goes away completely—you can begin to work on the technique itself."

If you're interested in one of these mock assault courses, I recommend that you attend one of their free public graduations so you can watch women fighting "model muggers." Just watching these women fight and talk about their experiences may make you realize that you, too, are capable of redirecting your fears and learning how to fight back.

Another self-defense course I recommend is Krav Maga (pronounced krahv ma-GAW), the official self-defense technique of the Israeli Defense Forces, antiterrorist units, and various branches of the Israeli National Police Forces. Relatively new to the United States, Krav Maga (in Hebrew it means "contact combat") is a system of down and dirty aggressive street fighting.

Krav Maga's eighty-one-year-old founder, Imi Lichtenfeld, was born in Bratislava, Czechoslovakia. A champion wrestler, boxer, gymnast, and son of the chief martial arts instructor of the Czech national police force, Lichtenfeld fought off Nazi Youth gang members in the 1930s, using a variety of moves, many of which wouldn't have been permitted in either the boxing ring or on the wrestling mat. After emigrating to Israel in 1942, he joined the Hagana and taught soldiers self-defense and later refined those teachings into the system he now calls Krav Maga. Today, Lichtenfeld stresses prevention of injury rather than promotion of violence. His motto is "May you be so good at defending yourself that you never have to kill."

Krav Maga doesn't use mock attackers like Model Mugging and IMPACT do. Instead, students fight each other, practicing real choke holds and learning how to swiftly break them. They also learn how to block and return punches. Although I have not taken Krav Maga, I've known people who have. "We're taught to hit where it hurts," one student says, "where there are no muscles to defend the body—places like the groin, head, and feet."

Krav Maga classes are held in southern California, Philadelphia, Boston, and New York, as well as France, Germany, Eng-

A woman thrusting the heel of her foot into the mugger's stomach.

A woman performing an axe kick to the mugger's head.

land, South Africa, and Australia. In Israel, classes are taught to adult civilians as well as children.

If your city does not have Krav Maga, Model Mugging, or IMPACT chapters, pursue other types of karate courses in your area, but find a program that emphasizes self-defense. Before joining, watch a class, and check whether there are women students. If they are segregated and sparring only with each other, I wouldn't recommend taking the class. You want to be able to spar with men.

If you don't want to take a self-defense course, I have a few suggestions I can give you, but remember these suggestions are only a minimal guide to fighting back: If I was attacked, the first thing I would do is yell "No!" and drop to the ground. Sounds strange? Maybe, but by dropping to the ground, I am reducing the disparity of height between the attacker and me. I want him to come down to my level so I can use my legs and feet to kick him because I know from mock fighting that I don't have the upper body strength to hurt him.

You may ask, why not kick him in the groin? Well, first, it's not so easy. If I'm standing and try to kick him, he'll probably grab my ankle and pull my legs out from under me, forcing me to fall hard on my back or even my head. That's why most self-defense experts advise you not to kick, but to use your knee when going for the groin. Unfortunately, however, that means you have to be very close to your attacker, which also poses certain problems.

So, in many ways, you're better off on the ground. The truth is, you'll probably be there pretty quickly anyway, because as I said before, when a woman is attacked, she is usually knocked to the ground in six seconds or less. When you're in the ground position, there are two types of kicking techniques you can use. The first is the axe kick, where you're on your back and you strike down with your heel. To use the second technique, you have to lie on your side and use your whole foot, thrusting out through your heel. If you want to practice these moves in your home, I recommend placing a big pillow on the floor and imagining that you're kicking an attacker's head and body. Don't worry about form. Remember, you're practicing to knock out the attacker. Get angry. If swearing helps to put you in an angry state, swear. Again, this doesn't come close to what you experience when taking a mock assault class, but I know women who have practiced these exercises at home and were later successful in fending off an attack.

Learning how to fight back—whether it's verbal self-defense or physical self-defense—is crucial to your empowerment, especially in these times when you may be the target of some person's aggressive behavior. Knowing self-defense techniques offers you more options to take care of yourself.

CHAPTER EIGHT

Can You Handle a Weapon?

FOR MOST ADULT women, the idea of owning a weapon and knowing how to use it is a foreign concept. Growing up, we did not participate in the BB gun and dirt clod wars our brothers were waging with their friends, nor did we have contests to see who could punch each other hardest in the shoulder. What did we know about fighting? Not much. "Boys have balls between their legs," my best friend, Karen, told me in fifth grade. "My daddy told me to kick them there if a boy bothers me. He says it hurts." That was what fighting meant to me. A swift kick in the balls and run. So consider yourself lucky if you played with any of your brothers' toy weapons. You're probably one step ahead of many women in knowing how to use a real weapon.

More than anything, the decision to carry a weapon is vital to your own personal vision because carrying a weapon gives you more parity with a potential attacker. Besides carrying it with you at all times, you must know how to use it. It's easy to *buy* Mace, pepper spray, a mini-baton, or even a gun, but it takes a certain commitment to learn how to use your weapon so well that you have no problem defending yourself with it in a crisis situation.

I wish weapons could make us invincible, but they don't.

They can help you in a fight. That's because weapons are extensions of your own fighting ability and can bolster your chances for success. But at the same time, it's important to recognize the limits of a weapon and to be aware when not to use it. For example, if a man is pointing a gun at you, you don't want to spray him with pepper spray, because he has lethal force and you don't. Also, you should only use your weapon if you are in fear of grave bodily harm or death or a loved one is in danger. If someone is stealing your computer, stereo, or best china, let him take it. There are other ways of being a hero.

I wish I could tell you that there are a whole range of weapons out there for you to chose from. In reality, apart from guns, your choices are limited to a mini-baton and personal defense sprays, though I will discuss other options. I keep both of these weapons in my purse, and I sometimes even walk down the street with one or the other in my hand, ready to use. Does that sound paranoid? I don't think so. Five years ago, I might have thought I was being overly cautious, but not today. I've just heard too many frightening stories from both women and men.

Nonlethal Weapons

Tear Gas

Most of us think of tear gas as something the police shoot out of a bazooka-like cannon to break up demonstrations or to flush criminals out of buildings they are holed up in. But in reality, anyone can buy this anticrime weapon, and you don't need to know how to fire a bazooka to use it.

First developed for use by the military in World War I, tear gas is a chlorine compound derived from either chloropicrin or nitrochloroform, which, when inhaled, causes acute tearing and temporary eye pain with other side effects that include confusion, nausea, and vomiting.

All that may sound great, because that's just how you'd like to make an attacker feel, but unfortunately tear gas has its disadvantages, and I dissuade people from using it. Though you can buy it in small, conveniently sized canisters (there are numerous brands), when you spray it, it has the tendency to spread and can end up affecting you as well as the attacker, especially if you spray it into a head wind.

Another problem is that while tear gas produces eyelid and nasal tissue pain, such pain often isn't enough to stop an attacker, especially one who is on drugs, which can dull the senses to pain and give an attacker superhuman strength. I've been told by police officers that some criminals actually tear gas each other to build up a tolerance against the chemical so they can resist police force. Like cockroaches, they gradually become immune to the spray and have to be attacked with higher doses and greater amounts. As a result, more and more police departments are giving up tear gas and using red pepper spray instead.

Red Pepper Spray

Far more effective than tear gas, red pepper spray is designed to incapacitate an attacker *instantly* without aftereffects. The product is sold under different brands and comes in different-sized canisters and formulas. Some are made by reliable companies; others aren't. One of the best is Best Defense pepper spray, a nonflammable, nontoxic, biodegradable spray that is used by more than 4,000 police departments.

Red pepper spray contains an oleoresin capsicum solution, an all-natural substance, better known as cayenne pepper, which is derived from various red pepper plants. When sprayed properly—whether in a stream or cone of mist or in burst units—it has devastating short-term effect on humans, regardless of their physical or emotional condition. The pepper causes the membranes to swell, producing instant eye closure, uncontrollable coughing, gagging, and the sensation of intense burning to the skin. It also forces the diaphragm to contract, which, in turn, causes the attacker to double over, often stopping him in his tracks.

You may know what it's like to accidentally bite into a red pepper or have one irritate your skin. It's not a pleasant experience. Well, imagine a pain ten times worse, and you'll know what it's like to get hit by pepper spray. Just ask Joe Boland, a former Denver police officer, who had to be pepper-sprayed as part of his training. "Getting hit with red pepper is like putting your hand on a hot stove and not being able to take it off," he says. "The pain keeps intensifying."

However, Boland says it's important to spray the attacker's face. Ideally, you want to be four to six feet away from your target when you spray him because if you get too close, the possibility exists that the spray will not mix properly, which can retard the full effect of the active agent for as long as thirty seconds, and that's much too long when you're being assaulted.

So like tear gas, pepper spray also has its limitations. If you're outside and the wind is blowing in your direction, the spray may affect you instead of your attacker. Used indoors, the spray might disable everyone! Recently, I heard a story about a man in a Beverly Hills restaurant who was showing his pepper spray canister to his dinner companion when he accidentally pushed the button and sent a stream into the air. Within minutes, people began to cough uncontrollably, and shortly afterward, the restaurant had to be evacuated.

When the spray has been discharged indoors, normal ventilation will remove it in forty-five minutes. If, for some reason, you accidentally get sprayed or spray yourself, your best bet is to get some fresh air, flush your eyes with cool water, and wash your entire body and hair with soap and water. However, even if you don't do anything, you should recover in fifteen to forty-five minutes. If you don't, call a doctor. After you feel up to it, check your clothes, and dump anything that's been sprayed into the washer or send it to the dry cleaners.

It's important to take a training class if it's available in your community. Although you'll be taught with spray canisters filled with water, you can still develop a sense of how accurately you can spray an attacker and at what distance. If there isn't a class in your area, purchase an inert canister (some companies sell an inert canister for the same price as a regular one), and practice spraying a friend, but don't turn it into a squirt-gun fight. Take

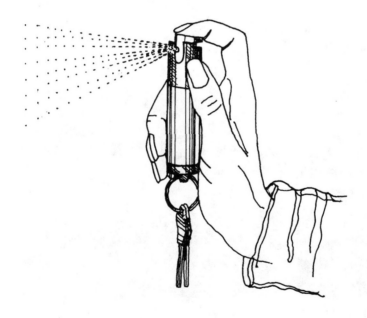

One of the best ways to carry a pepper spray canister is on your key chain. If you feel you're unsafe, carry the canister in your strong hand in the ready position.

it seriously. If you plan to use the canister as a key chain, as many are equipped to be, practice with keys on the ring, and rehearse various scenarios, including attacking each other from

The Hidden Edge Siren & Safety Spray is equipped with a 130-decibel siren and an environmentally safe pepper spray. If it is ever grabbed away from you, the unit's special safety pin feature automatically disarms the spray to prevent it from being turned against you.

behind. Also, practice pulling the canister out of your pocket or purse and make sure you get a feel for the canister so you'll be able to tell which way the nozzle is pointed without having to look at it. Soon, you'll have a pretty good idea of how you'll react in a crisis situation.

When walking outdoors or in a potentially dangerous location, I recommend that you make it a habit to carry your canister in your strong hand in a ready position. Once an attack begins, it becomes extremely difficult to get to the spray if it's tucked away in a purse or pocket. As soon as you perceive a threat, place your thumb on the canister's actuator and get ready to push down on it.

Then it happens. The guy who's been following you makes a rush at you, and you hold up the canister and spray him in the face. What happens next? Does he fall into a heap, moaning, while you watch? Not necessarily. In fact, he may do the opposite: He may react in a deranged and violent way, which is why Massad Ayoob, who trains police officers in the use of sprays, recommends that you simulate worst-case scenarios during training. Practice moving side to side like a boxer and spraying the attacker's face again. According to Ayoob, "It is important to move because if the attacker carries on his assault, he most probably will strike toward the position where he last saw you."

Once he goes down, get away from him. If you are near a public place, go there and notify someone to call the police. Or if you get in your car and drive away, drive to a safe place and use a phone to call the police.

Be careful what brand you buy. There are over 100 pepper sprays on the market. As I said earlier, canisters are available in different sizes and can be purchased at hardware and gun stores or through catalogs. But make sure the canister you buy contains a minimum of ten seconds worth of spray and at least 10 percent oleoresin capsicum. This information should be stated in the manufacturer's instructions.

Furthermore, be aware that as of this writing, pepper spray is illegal in Hawaii and New York City; in Nevada, you have to take a class and in California you need to watch a video, before you are allowed to carry it. Another warning: Although you can take tear gas and pepper spray canisters across state lines, it is not a good idea to take these products on planes, even in checked luggage, because increased air pressure at high altitudes can cause the canisters to leak and destroy your clothes and cosmetics. I suggest you buy a canister at your destination point, and if you don't use it, give it to someone as a present when you leave.

If you choose to throw it out, be careful where you dispose of it. You don't want a child to find a filled canister and use it. The same rule applies when you are at home around your own children. Make sure you keep the canister out of their reach. If you think this will be a problem, then I would discourage you from purchasing a spray product.

Mini-batons

A mainstay of personal protection tools is the mini-baton, also known as a Kubotan. Simple in construction, a Kubotan is a solid plastic, ribbed dowel three and a half inches long and three-eighths of an inch in diameter with a key chain attached to one end. Designed by a leading martial arts instructor, Shihan Tahuyuki Kubota, the mini-baton is used by the police, prison guards, and other law enforcement personnel.

When you first see one, it's hard to imagine that it can be an effective defense weapon, but watch someone who really knows how to use it, and you'll be amazed by how devastating it can be. I was fortunate enough to meet Kubota in his Glendale, California, studio, where he taught me various wrist and necklock takedowns as well as how to use the baton to slash an attacker's face and eyes. The only problem was—and I told

Carry your mini-baton in your strong hand while walking or wait-ing for public transportation. A mini-baton acts as both a deterrent and a weapon.

Kubota this—it would have taken me many weeks, if not months, of practice to master the defensive moves he showed me in his four-hour training session. "Yes," he said, agreeing, "you must practice these techniques. They are not easy. But they are very good to know once you learn them."

He's right—they are good to know. But if you don't have the time or the money to go through the training, you can still use the mini-baton as a deterrent because just its presence makes a statement. For example, when I walk along the street or in parking lots, malls, and other public places, I carry it in my strong hand with my keys noisily dangling down from the end of it. I've noticed many people, especially men, eyeing it cautiously, and sometimes a person who seems intent on approaching me will shy away from me at the last moment. In an elevator one day, one man asked me whether I was an off-duty police officer. "I've seen cops carrying those," he said. "I'm not a cop," I told him, "but I've been trained by the police." He didn't say anything after that.

Besides functioning as a deterrent, the mini-baton is a symbol to its owner. One of my students told me that when she holds her mini-baton, it prompts her to be aware of her surroundings. "It's just a good reminder," she says. "It keeps you on your toes."

It also makes your keys very easy to find in your purse. However, it can cause problems while you're driving. With your keys in the ignition, you might find the bottom of the mini-baton knocking into the top of your leg or clanging against the side of the steering column. So what I do is stick an extra set of my car keys on a small key chain that I use when I drive and the rest of my keys, including a second set of car keys, I keep on my mini-baton. When I park, and have to give my car keys to an attendant, I just give him the small key chain and put my mini-baton in my purse or carry it in my hand.

Plastic mini-batons are legal to carry in the United States and come in a variety of colors, though black, I think, is the most intimidating. They can be purchased for under $10 at gun stores and through mail services. You shouldn't have a problem taking one through airport security unless it's made of metal. Those can be confiscated, so beware.

Stun Guns

Not to be confused with the futuristic weapons used by the fictitious characters in "Star Trek" and *Star Wars,* stun guns do not have the ability to fire bolts of energy great distances. In fact, you don't shoot anything out of a stun gun, you simply turn it on to generate anywhere from 25,000 to 100,000 volts, depending on the gun. It doesn't offer the distance defense that pepper spray does, because you can only use it if your attacker is right next to you.

A stun gun will only work if you manage to firmly press the gun's small electrodes against the attacker's body while holding down the trigger button for up to four seconds. Frankly, I don't know of any assailant who will allow his victim to do that. Also, there is no guarantee that an attacker will be fully affected by the charge. One rape victim told me how the man who attacked her was immune to the electricity from her stun gun. Why? Because he had been electrocuted before, she later found out. "He took the gun away from me," she said, "and electrocuted me." Clearly, that is one of dangers of using the gun. If your attacker doesn't become immediately incapacitated, there is a good chance he will take the gun away and use it against you.

What exactly does a stun gun do? After it makes electrical contact with a person's body, it overrides the nervous system, causing severe, uncontrollable muscle spasms and temporary paralysis. If it works, an attacker will drop to the ground and stay there, weak and dazed, for up to fifteen minutes, giving you a chance to run away. Rarely does a charge cause cardiac arrest.

Over the last five years, I've talked to several women who have used stun guns, and the overall consensus seems to be that they are more useful as a deterrent than a weapon. For example, if you are in an underground parking lot and you feel threatened by someone coming toward you, you can warn him to stay away by holding your stun gun up and pushing the trigger button. Instantly, a bright blue bolt of electricity will crackle across the electrodes, like a minibolt of lighting. That sight alone, which is quite impressive in a dimly lit area, can stop a person from coming any closer.

Stun guns are available in assorted sizes and voltages and can be purchased in gun stores. They are not legal in all states, so check with your local police department before purchasing one.

Improvised Weapons

Almost wherever you are, there are objects nearby that can be used as self-defense weapons. Just look around your house, and you'll see that if you are suddenly attacked, you may be able to use a desk lamp, wooden hanger, book, pot, or any other heavy small object as a weapon. If you are out on the street or in the wilderness, think about throwing a rock, stones, dirt, or sand in your assailant's face. But be aware that these improvised weapons may not stop the assailant and could be taken away and used against you.

Baseball Bats

Some people recommend that women keep baseball bats under their beds or in their cars. If the bat is made of wood, you can drill screws or hammer nails into it to make an even better weapon. But there are a couple of problems you should be aware of. First, you really need to take a good swing in order to deliver an effective blow. Generally, this requires the use of both hands and a fair amount of upper body and arm strength, attributes most women don't have unless they lift weights. Second, because a bat is long, you might have a hard time retrieving it quickly from under your bed or car seat. Third, it can easily be taken away from you.

Some women play softball and go to the batting cages and take whacks just like men, but unless you feel you can deliver a solid shot—and I don't mean a little dribbler to the second baseman—I don't recommend a baseball bat as an effective user-friendly weapon.

Flashlights

Even though a flashlight's main function is to assist you in the dark, a big black flashlight—a police flashlight, which is made of anodized aircraft aluminum and packed with C or D cell batteries—is one of the most effective improvised weapons you can use. It also reminds some criminals of their encounters with the police, which makes it a good deterrent.

If you are attacked, a flashlight is not only a good weapon to strike someone with, but you can use it to block blows, especially if you know any martial arts. Remember, though, that a police flashlight can kill someone, and in most states, the law considers blows to the head with a flashlight lethal force. That means you should only strike an assailant's skull in a situation where your life is in danger or you fear grave bodily harm, which includes rape.

To practice using your flashlight as a weapon, hit it against a utility pole or another solid object so you know how it feels to strike something. Then try to turn it on afterward. I think you'll find that it can withstand punishment.

Rolled-Up Magazines, Books, Notebooks, and Clipboards

A tightly rolled-up magazine (preferably secured with thick rubber bands) can offer some protection if you surprise the attacker by jabbing him.

One way is to jab downward with the butt end of the rolled-up magazine. Police officer and self-defense instructor Massad Ayoob recommends that a right-handed woman swing the magazine up over her left shoulder and then strike down as hard she can, aiming for the assailant's throat. But he cautions that this windup offers the attacker an opportunity to block or seize the magazine. As an alternative, he suggests simply jabbing forward to the throat, using both hands, pole-vault style. If you're right-handed, put your right hand on the rear of the magazine, palm down on top, and your left hand, palm up, under the front of it. But unless you surprise him, there's a good chance he'll deflect your blow or even grab the magazine in midair and take it away from you.

Hard-bound books, notebooks, and clipboards can also hurt an attacker. If you're holding one of these makeshift weapons against your chest, you can slam the edge into the criminal's throat, aiming for his Adam's apple, but be ready to fight or run. Unless you've knocked him out, he'll probably take the object away and strike you with it.

Hair Spray and Paint Spray

Keep your hair spray and paint spray at home since they only cause momentary stinging of the eyes and do very little harm to an assailant. Of course, if that's all you have at your disposal when you're being attacked, by all means, use it. But know the spray's limitations and be ready to fight, scream, and run.

Umbrellas, Walking Sticks, and Canes

An umbrella is used to protect you from the rain, not from predators. Unless it's a very expensive model, it's going to be pretty flimsy and won't do you much good. Just like a rough storm, an attacker can easily snatch your umbrella and rip it apart within seconds, so I only recommend using it as a last resort.

Similarly, if you use a walking stick, which few of us do, I don't recommend using it as a weapon unless you're trained in the martial art of stick-fighting. For handicapped people or seniors who use a cane, I only have this advice: If you're attacked, don't try to use your cane as a club since its impact will not stop an attacker. Instead, when you see the assailant coming toward you (and hopefully you'll have time to react), slip the cane up the inside of your forearm so that the staff is at the bottom of your strong hand. If you decide to fight, hold your cane-fortified arm across your chest and whack down on your attacker's arms and wrists. You may fracture some bones and cause him considerable pain without really hurting yourself. It doesn't sound easy and it isn't, but you'd be surprised at how many cane-wielding seniors have successfully warded off their attackers using just this method.

Keys, Nail Files, Eyeglasses, and Hat Pins

Poking your attacker in the eye with a key, nail file, hat pin, or the arm of a pair of eyeglasses sounds good in theory, but these "weapons" are inadequate in most situations. The problem is that when you're in a high-adrenaline state, you tend to lose your small-motor abilities. For example, if you're holding your keys between your fingers inside a clenched fist, unless you're a trained boxer, you'll probably lose your keys once you start fighting. As I've said before, use any of these objects as a last resort, but my best advice is to keep your keys on your mini-baton.

Should You Own a Gun?

A gun is an effective deterrent and provides what I call *distance defense*. No other weapon—stun gun, pepper spray, or mini-baton—gives the victim the power to stop an attacker at a distance before he assaults her.

However, owning a gun is a tremendous responsibility. It is a lethal weapon that can change your life as well as many others in an instant. That's why, if you decide to own one, you need to treat it with the respect it deserves. That means taking a gun in-

struction class from a professional—preferably an instructor
certified by the National Rifle Association—and then returning
monthly to the gun range to practice the skills you learned. It
also means making sure that you store your gun in a secure
place, preferably a safe, where young children can't get to it.
(See the appendix for two good gun storage units.)

Gun ownership isn't for everyone. If you live in a house
where someone is depressed, suicidal, violent, or abuses alcohol or drugs, then I don't recommend having a gun in your
home. Also, if you don't know whether you'll be able to shoot
an attacker if you or one of your loved ones is attacked, then
you shouldn't own a gun. In a crisis situation, if you can't pull
the trigger, your gun could be taken away from you and used
against you, which is the ultimate tragedy.

Most of us are aware that there are studies that show the
dangers of owning a handgun as well as studies that show the
benefits of owning a handgun. But many people aren't aware
that when a gun is used in self-defense, the vast majority of the
time it is never fired. "Often, just showing your gun to an attacker is good enough to scare him away," I tell my students,
citing a study done by Gary Kleck, a professor of criminology at
Florida State University. Kleck's study shows that Americans
use guns in self-defense about a million times a year, but only
fire their weapons in 4 percent of those incidents.

Unfortunately, the media isn't all that interested in the incidents where people ward off their attackers by simply display-
ing their guns. To make the papers, you have to shoot someone
or be shot yourself. Although that's understandable, I also think
credit needs to be given to the millions of women and men who
have successfully defended themselves without firing their
guns.

Purchasing a Gun

If you're considering buying a gun for self-protection, I recommend that you take a gun training class first so that you can try out various models. There are hundreds of different sizes of handguns, and you need to find one that fits comfortably in your hand and you can shoot accurately. To your surprise, you may find it easier to shoot a large-framed .357 Magnum than a small-framed .38 Special.

I recommend that you own a revolver rather than a semiautomatic for the following reasons:

- It is easier to load and unload bullets from a revolver.
- It is easier to tell if a revolver is loaded or unloaded.
- It is easier to clean a revolver. You need to clean a gun every time it is shot.
- A revolver is less likely to jam. Semiautomatics can jam and if you aren't quick to clear the jam, the gun is useless.

Revolvers come in many different caliber sizes. For self-defense, you need a gun that will stop an attacker. A .38 Special or a .357 Magnum has good stopping power, especially with dependable factory-loaded ammunition. There are many different gun manufacturers, both American and foreign. Guns vary in prices and generally cost between $200 and $600.

I am a spokesperson for Smith & Wesson, one of the oldest and largest gun manufacturers in the world, and I recommend their products, which have service policies. Smith & Wesson produces a line called the LadySmith, which is designed for women. My gun of choice for home self-defense is the .357 Magnum LadySmith Model 65. Another model that I like and have personally endorsed is the .38 Special Model 640, which has been handcrafted by the gunsmiths at Smith & Wesson's world-reknowned Performance Center. This edition features a fully compensated barrel that is designed to reduce recoil when firing the gun. Also, the revolver's action has been tuned for a smooth, consistent trigger pull, and the rosewood grip is specifically sized for a woman's hand.

Carrying a Handgun

Some of you may want to carry a gun on you or in your car. You should be aware that many states require a permit to carry a concealed weapon, and in some states, it is totally illegal to do so. In some regions of the United States, it's legal to transport a firearm from state to state in a car, so check state laws. If you're traveling by plane, you are allowed to store your unloaded gun in a locked container in a checked suitcase. You have to declare that you have a gun and show the check-in attendant how it is stored. Every airline's policy differs so call ahead to find out the carrier's procedures.

If you decide to carry a gun and you've complied with your state's laws, I recommend that you take a gun combat course. You'll find once you leave your home with your gun, the conditions for shooting it become much more complicated.

Men usually carry their guns in a belt or shoulder holster, but women have a wide variety of choices, including specially designed purses, waist packs, and briefcases that keep their gun separate from other items and make it easy to access.

Shotguns for Home Self-Defense

I have never mastered the recoil from a shotgun, so I haven't felt comfortable recommending a shotgun for home self-defense. But there are many firearm experts who say that a shotgun is an excellent weapon for safe room home defense. Depending on the ammunition and range, a shotgun has higher stopping power and is easier to aim than a handgun. However, it has a couple of drawbacks. One problem is most women have to use two hands to shoot it. Another is it can be difficult to store in a safe and be accessible in an emergency situation.

If you are interested in owning a shotgun for home self-protection, take a shotgun class and try 12-gauge and 20-gauge pump and semiautomatic shotguns. Some women are very proficient shotgun shooters and prefer them over handguns.

Gun Control Laws

There are federal gun control laws as well as state and city laws. So, before purchasing a gun for self-protection, I suggest that you find out the laws that apply to your area. Your local police department or your state National Rifle Association will give you the information you need to know. Just remember, whatever gun you buy, you, and not anybody else, are responsible for gun safety in your home.

APPENDICES

Organizations and Instruction

The Law Enforcement
   Alliance of America
Brenda Maples, president
(800) 766-8578

National Rifle Association
11250 Waples Mill Road
Fairfax, VA 22030
(800) 645-4NRA

Protect Safe Run
   (dog escorts)
Dianne Witt
4325 N.E. Thompson
Portland, OR 97213

Scotti School (car-driving
   school)
11 Riverside Avenue,
   Suite 15
Medford, MA 02155
(800) 343-0046

Second Amendment
   Foundation
12500 N.E. Tenth Place
Bellevue, WA 98005
(800) 426-4302

United Schutzhund Clubs
   of America
   (dog training)
729 Lemay Ferry Road
St. Louis, MO 63125
(314) 638-9686

We are AWARE (Arming
   Women Against Rape
   and Endangerment)
P.O. Box 255
Maynard, MA 01754
(508) 443-5404

Women Refusing to Accept
   Tenant Harassment
   (WRATH)

607 Elmira Rd., Suite 299
Vacaville, CA 95687
(707) 449-1122

SELF-DEFENSE COURSES

IMPACT Personal Safety and
Model Mugging chapters

CALIFORNIA:
San Francisco

BAMM/Impact
1561 Industrial Way
San Carlos, CA 94070
(415) 592-7300

San Luis Obispo

Model Mugging of SLO
P.O. Box 986
San Luis Obispo, CA
93406
(805) 544-KICK

Santa Rosa

CORE Dynamics
P.O. Box 12206
Santa Rosa, CA 95406
(707) 544-CORE

Los Angeles

Matthew Thomas
Model Mugging
859 N. Hollywood Way,
#127
Burbank, CA 91505
(818) 988-0345

IMPACT Personal Safety
19301 Ventura Boulevard,
#200
Tarzana, CA 91356
(800) 345-KICK

ILLINOIS
Chicago

The Self Empowerment
Group
P.O. Box 597094
Chicago, IL 60659
(312) 338-4545

MASSACHUSETTS
Boston

Model Mugging of Boston
1168 Commonwealth
Avenue
Boston, MA 02134
(617) 232-7900

MINNESOTA
Minneapolis/St. Paul

IMPACT of Minnesota
P.O. Box 47052
Plymouth, MN 55447
(612) 475-4008

MISSOURI
Kansas City

Mid-America Model
Mugging
4030 Broadway,
Kansas City, MO 64111
(816) 931-8022

NEW YORK
New York City (tristate area)

IMPACT/Prepare Inc.
25 West 43rd Street, #2100
New York, NY 10036
(800) 442-PARE or
(212) 719-5800

Resources for Personal
Empowerment
P.O. Box 20316
New York, NY 10028
(800) 443-KICK

OREGON
Portland

Model Mugging of Portland
4326 S.E. Woodstock, #434
Portland, OR 97206
(503) 243-1296

CANADA
Montreal (Quebec)

Aggression Simulee
Boite Postal 36
Succursale DeLorimier
Montreal, H2H-2N6,
Quebec, Canada
(514) 528-1396

Vancouver

Model Mugging of
Vancouver
2945 W. 16th Avenue
Vancouver, V6K-3CV
British Columbia,Canada
(604) 623-2395

VERMONT
Burlington

Model Mugging of
Vermont
P.O. Box 194
Burlington, VT 05402
(802) 860-8410

WASHINGTON
Seattle
Powerful Choices
P.O. Box 30918
Seattle, WA 98103
(206) 782-5662

WASHINGTON, DC
DC IMPACT
701 Richmond Avenue
Silver Spring, MD 20910
(301) 589-1349

SWITZERLAND
IMPACT SWITZERLAND
(ZURICH)

Bergstrasse 21, CH8113
Boppelsen, Switzerland
011-41-1-845-0580

Chapman Academy Practical
Shooting (handgun training)
Ray Chapman
Route 1, Box 27A
Hallsville, MO 65255
(314) 696-5544

Defensive Training, Inc.
John Farnam
P.O. Box 665
Niwot, CO 80544
(303) 530-7106

Executive Security International (bodyguard school)
P.O. Box 80
Basalt, CO 81621
(800) 847-0888

Krav Maga Association
P.O. 8723
Calabasas, CA 91372
(818) 501-6510

Lethal Force Institute
(handgun training)
Massad Ayoob
P.O. Box 122
Concord, NH 03301
(603) 224-6814

Los Angeles Commission on
Assaults Against Women
543 North Fairfax Avenue
Los Angeles, CA 90036
(213) 651-3147

Paxton Quigley's Women's
Empowerment in the '90s
Seminar
9903 Santa Monica Boulevard, Suite 300
Beverly Hills, CA 90212
(310) 281-1762

RESOURCES

CAMPSITE SECURITY PRODUCTS
Battery-Operated Motion Detector

Detec Security Systems, Inc.
927 Calle Negocio, Suite A
San Clemente, CA. 92673
(714) 366-9391

HOME SECURITY PRODUCTS
Door Stopper

The Door Jammer
price: $29.95
Intertrade Marketing
2145 Resort Drive, #204
P.O. Box 5164
Steamboat Springs, CO
80477
(800) 800-1011

Home Automation System

Intelligent Home
Controller
price: $1,000
Mastervoice
17059 El Cajon Avenue
Yorba Linda, CA 92686
(714) 524-4488

Wireless Home Alarm System

Snif Safestart System
price, (basic unit): $389
560-5600 Parkwood Way
Richmond, British
Columbia, V6V-2M2,
Canada
(604) 273-7643

Closed Circuit Television:

EO-1242C Observation
System
price: $400
EXXIS
1220 Champion Circle,
#100
Carrollton, TX 75006
(800) 68-EXXIS

Barking Dog Alarm

The Safety Zone Catalog
price: $129.95
(800) 999-3030

Escape Rope Ladder

The Res-Q-Ladder
price: $69.95 to $99.95
The Safety Zone Catalog
(800) 999-3030

**Wireless Solar Powered
Security Light**

Siemens Solar Sensor
Light
price: $169.95
The Safety Zone Catalog
(800) 999-3030

PERSONAL SAFETY ALARMS,
SPRAY DEVICES, AND MINI-
BATONS

Siren And Spray Device

Hidden Edge Siren &
Spray
price: $49.95
860 Cottage Hill Avenue,
Sky Ranch
Mobile, AL 36693
(800) 513-1984

Mini-baton

Paxton's Mini-Baton
price: $12.95
Paxton Quigley
Enterprises, Inc.
9903 Santa Monica
Boulevard,
Suite 300
Beverly Hills, CA 90212
(310) 281-1762

Paxton Quigley's Personal
Protection Pak
(mini-baton, pepper
spray, and book)
price: $21.95
(800) 800-1011

Pepper Spray

Best Defense Pepper
Spray
price: $9.95 and up
(various sizes)
2145 Resort Drive,
Suite 204
P.O. Box 5164
Steamboat Springs, CO
80477
(800) 800-1011

Bulletproof Vests, (Various models)

price: $265

MPS Company
1441 John Street
Matthew, NC 28106
(704) 847-8793

Wallets

Colloc Wallet (a "minisafe"
that sprays indelible
ink on the wallet's con-
tents when tampered
with, has a four-digit
combination lock)
price: $89
Hermelin Inc.
3100 Airway Avenue, #119
Costa Mesa, CA 92626

(800) 545-4808

CAR PRODUCTS
Steering Wheel Device

The Claw
price: $49.95
Anes/Code Alarm
(800) ASK-ANES

Car Disabling System

The Immobilock (shuts
down up to four essen-
tial electric systems)
price: $400
Securalock Systems
3828 North 28th Avenue
Phoenix, AZ 85017
(602) 230-9000

Auto & Stereo Alarm
price: $49.95
Intertrade Marketing
2145 Resort Drive
Suite 204
Steamboat Springs, CO
80477
(800) 800-1011

GUN SAFETY PRODUCTS

Children's Safety Program

Eddie Eagle Safety
   Program
price: free
National Rifle Association
11250 Waples Mill Road
Fairfax, VA 22030
(800) 231-0752

Large Home Safes

Fire King International,
   Inc.
price: various models
101 Security Parkway
New Albany, IN 47150
(800) 457-2424

Small Gun Safes (Available at Gun Stores)

The Buck Security Box
   (can't be permanently
   mounted)
price: $65
4338 West Highway 82
P.O. Box 973
Gainesville, TX 76241
(800) 582-2825

PistolPal
price: $125 to $299
   (various models)
PistolPal Products

2930 North Campbell
   Avenue
Chicago, IL 60618
(800) 788-7725

MAGAZINES

Women & Guns (gives in-
   formation on guns,
   sport shooting, gun-re-
   lated products, and all
   forms of self-defense
   for women)
12500 N.W. Tenth Place
Bellevue, WA 98005
(206) 454-7012

Safe & Secure Living (gives
   product information
   and advice on making
   your life safer and
   more secure)
P.O. Box 16149
North Hollywood, CA
   91606
(818) 760-8983

Women's Self Defense (provides product informa-
   tion, news on legislation,
   as well as discussions on
   all aspects of self-defense, how to deal with
   confrontations, etc.)

Spectrum Building
4901 N.W. 17th Way, #600
Fort Lauderdale, FL
    33309
(305) 772-2788

The Safety Zone Catalog
    (excellent source for
    home safety and per-
    sonal protection prod-
    ucts)
The Safety Zone
Hanover, PA 17333-0019
(800) 999-3030

INVESTIGATIVE SERVICE:

Intelligence Inc.(Good
    source for locating peo-
    ple, background
    checks, business credit,
    divorce searches, crim-
    inal records, etc. Ask
    for the catalog.)
2228 South El Camino
    #349
San Mateo, CA 94403
FAX: 415-851-5403

BIBLIOGRAPHY

Ayoob, Massad, *The Truth About Self-Protection,* Bantam Books, New York, 1988.

Bates, Lyn, "Why Is It in Vogue to Fear Guns?" *Women & Guns,* January, 1994.

Birnbaum, J., and N. Groth, *Men Who Rape: The Psychology of the Offender,* Plenum Press, New York, 1979.

Braunig, Martha, *Executive Protection Bible,* E.S.I. Education Development Corporation, Aspen, CO, 1994.

Cameron, Deborah, and Elizabeth Frazer, *The Lust to Kill,* New York University Press, New York, 1987.

Cleary, Thomas (translated from Huanchu Daoren), *Back to Beginnings; Reflections on the Tao,* Shambhala, Boston, 1990.

Cleary, Thomas, *The Japanese Art of War,* Shambhala, Boston, 1992.

Cooper, Jeff, *Principles of Personal Defense,* Paladin Press, Boulder, CO, 1972.

Cowley, Jeffrey, with Carol Hall, "The Genetics of Bad Behavior," *Newsweek,* November 1, 1993.

Coyne, John, "Violence: Special Hazard For Nurses," *Glamour,* October, 1993.

Estés, Clarissa Pinkola, *Women Who Run with the Wolves,* Ballantine Books, New York, 1992.

Friedman, Lawrence M., *Crime and Punishment in American History,* Basic Books, New York, 1993.

Gaeta, Lisa, *Women's Basics Course Workbook,* Impact Personal Safety, Van Nuys, CA 91402.

Hay, Vicky, "Don't Be a Victim,"

Real Estate Sales People,
March/April 1986.

Huber, Craig Fox, and Don Paul,
Secure from Crime, Path
Finder Publications, 1296 E.
Gibson Rd., #E-301, Wood-
land, CA 95776, 1994.

Kates, Don B., Jr., "Some Re-
marks on the Prohibition of
Handguns," *St. Louis University Law Journal,* Vol. 23,
1979.

Kinney, Joseph, A., and Dennis
Johnson, *Breaking Point—
The Employee Violence Epi-
demic,* National Safe
Workplace Institute, Court-
house Place, 54 W. Hubbard
St., #403, Chicago, IL 60610.

Kleck, Gary, *Point Blank: Guns
and Violence in America,* Aldine de Gruyter, Hawthorne,
NY, 1991.

Kubota, Takayuki, and John Pe-
ters, Jr., *Official Kubotan
Techniques,* Kubotan Institute, P.O. Box 14872 Station
G, N.E., Albuquerque, NM
87111, 1983.

Lanny, Roger, "Shotguns for
Home Defense," *Women &
Guns,* January, 1994.

Lipman, Ira A., *How to Protect
Yourself from Crime,* Con-
temporary Books, Chicago,
1989.

Mizell, Louis, Jr., *Street Sense*
for Women, Berkley, New
York, 1993.

Nelson, Joan, *Self-Defense, Steps
to Success,* Leisure Press,
Champaign, IL, 1993.

Paglia, Camille, *Sex, Art, and
American Culture,* Vintage,
New York, 1992.

Powers, Tim, and Richard Isaacs,
*The Seven Steps to Personal
Safety,* Center for Personal
Defense Studies, P.O. Box
2464, New York, NY, 10009-
8921.

Quigley, Paxton, *Armed &
Female,* St. Martin's Press,
New York, 1994.

Reynolds, Morgan, and W.W.
Caruth III, *Myths about Gun
Control,* National Center for
Policy Analysis, 12655 N.
Central Expressway, #720,
Dallas, TX 75243, 1993.

Scotti, Anthony, *Executive Safety
& International Terrorism,*
Prentice-Hall, Englewood
Cliffs, NJ, 1986.

Scotti, Anthony, *Police Driving
Techniques,* Prentice-Hall,
Englewood Cliffs, NJ, 1988.

Sennewald, Charles, and John
Christman, *Shoplifting,* But-
terworth-Heinemann Publishers, Stoneham, MA, 1993.

Silver, Carol, Ruth and Don B.
Kates Jr., unpublished study
reported in "Gun Control and

the Subway Class," *Wall
Street Journal,* January 10,
1985.

Toufexis, Anastasia, "Seeking the
Roots of Violence," *Time,*
April 19, 1993.

Turner, James T., *Handbook of
Hospital Security and Safety,*
Aspen Publications, Rockville,
MD, 1993.

Williamson, Marianne, *A Return
to Love,* Random House, New
York, 1993.

Wolf, Naomi, *Fire with Fire: The
New Female Power and How
It Will Change the Twenty-
First Century,* Random
House, New York, 1993.

Wright, James D., and Peter H.
Rossi, *Armed and Considered
Dangerous: A Survey of
Felons and Their Firearms,*
Aldine de Gruyter,
Hawthorne, NY, 1986.

INDEX

Page numbers in *italics* refer to captions.

ABOUT THE AUTHOR

PAXTON QUIGLEY is a nationally recognized personal safety authority and has taught more than 4,000 women personal protection strategies, including the use of a handgun. President of Paxton Quigley Enterprises, Inc., Beverly Hills, California, she is the author of the best-selling book, *Armed & Female* (New York: St. Martin's Press, 1994) and the first female spokesperson for Smith & Wesson. She is also a spokesperson for Pachmayr grips.

Miss Quigley has been leading seminars, Women's Empowerment in the '90s, for four years. No stranger to the media, she has appeared on more than 200 television and radio shows, including "60 Minutes," "The Today Show," "Good Morning America," "The Larry King Show," "The G. Gordon Liddy Show," and "NBC Nightly News" with Tom Brokaw.

She has been interviewed and widely quoted by the nation's leading newspapers, including the *New York Times*, the *Los Angeles Times*, the *Washington Post*, and the *Chicago Tribune*. She was also profiled on the front page of the *Wall Street Journal*. Her book was excerpted in *Glamour*, and she has been featured in *Elle, Mirabella, People, Health, Entrepreneur, MS*, and *Working Woman*.

About the Author

She is on the community advisory boards of IMPACT, AWARE, and SAVE.

Miss Quigley received her masters degree in anthropology from the University of Chicago and her bachelor's degree in speech from Northwestern University.